THE LIVING TEMPLE

THE
LIVING TEMPLE

George Herbert
and Catechizing

STANLEY FISH

Know ye not that ye are the temple of God?

University of California Press
Berkeley • Los Angeles • London

University of California Press
Berkeley and Los Angeles, California
University of California Press, Ltd.
London, England
Copyright © 1978 by
The Regents of the University of California
ISBN 0-520-02657-8
Library of Congress Catalog Card Number: 73-90664
Printed in the United States of America

1 2 3 4 5 6 7 8 9

For Jackson Cope

"Thy friend put in thy bosom . . ."

George Herbert,
The Church-porch

Contents

Acknowledgments

I WISH to thank the staffs of the Huntington Library, the Clark Library, and the Research Library of U.C.L.A. for the many courtesies extended to me during the preparation of this manuscript. I am grateful to the friends and colleagues who read the manuscript and who, by tempering their criticisms with praise, gently prompted me to the labors of revision. They are: Boyd Berry, Stephen Booth, Jackson Cope, Barbara Harman, Barbara Lewalski, Jerome McGann, Walter Michaels, Stephen Orgel, J. Max Patrick, Alan Roper, David Stam, Arnold Stein, Edward Weismiller, and Barry Weller. I owe a particular debt to Hugh Kenner, who, in an afternoon's conversation, told me how to write it. William Cain has provided invaluable editorial assistance from the first to the final drafts. And finally, I must acknowledge, once again, the patience of Adrienne Fish who remains, despite herself, the best proof-reader in the world.

One: Catechizing the Reader

1. ORDER OR SURPRISE: CRITICISM'S TWO HERBERTS

FOR MUCH of this century, the shape of Herbert criticism has been constrained by an obligatory comparison with the poetry of Donne. George Williamson's statement of 1930 is both typical and succinct:

In contrast to Donne, *The Temple* reveals a poet who has a spontaneous sincerity which permits a more direct approach to God, and a secure faith which, despite his sense of sin, brings him to acquiescence within the quiet shadow of the Church.[1]

Herbert, Williamson concludes, "lacks the gnawing remorse and lacerating passion of Donne"; he is "more at ease in Zion." In this poet of ease, security, and quiet one recognizes the holy and saintly Herbert of hagiographical tradition. That tradition has entered modern criticism by 1921 when Grierson describes *The Temple* as breathing "the spirit of the Anglican church at its best, primitive

---

1. *The Donne Tradition* (New York, Noonday Press edition, 1958), p. 100.

and modest,"[2] and it is very much in force in 1950 when
C. V. Wedgwood offers this tribute:

Herbert is one of those perfected personalities that always stand
apart from the blemished and friable majority of human beings.
He was a man of perfectly balanced goodness and his poetry
has a serenity which is already beyond passion. For that reason
he can never stir the emotions as Crashaw or Donne can stir
them.[3]

Indeed, the tradition is so strong that even a critic who
writes in reaction to it is in danger of being absorbed by it.
Helen White begins her influential essay by complaining
that "the picture which Walton draws of the gentle saint
of Bemerton may be a real bar to the appreciation of the
fiber of his spiritual life and the energy of his mind," and
she insists that "Herbert is no naive and innocent dévot,
singing with unpremeditated spontaneity."[4] But before
she concludes, Herbert has been found to begin "at a
point which Donne reached only after many painful
years," and described as feeling "no strain in his faith"
because "he knows where he is" (pp. 166, 168). As a
consequence, readers of his poetry also know where they
are, since "there is less of surprise in him than in most of
the metaphysicals, more of inevitability" (p. 185).

There are, of course, distinctions to be made between
White, Wedgwood, Williamson, and Grierson; but it is
fair, I think, to cite them as representatives of what was
once a consensus position, and it is a position that Helen
Vendler, writing in 1970, does not even feel obliged to

2. H. J. C. Grierson, *Metaphysical Lyrics & Poems of the Seventeenth
Century* (Oxford, 1921), p. xliv.

3. *Seventeenth-Century English Literature* (Oxford, 1950), p. 83.

4. *The Metaphysical Poets* (New York, Collier Books edition, 1962), pp.
145, 157.

consider. The opening sentences of her essay "The Re-invented Poem" boldly characterize a poet quite unlike the Herbert given us by an earlier criticism:

One of the particular virtues of Herbert's poetry is its extremely provisional quality. His poems are ready at any moment to change direction or to modify attitudes. Even between the title and the first line, Herbert may rethink his position.[5]

A survey of the current scene suggests that Professor Vendler's view now prevails and that the older view of a calm and resolute Herbert is no longer in fashion. Vendler is able to cite Valentina Poggi and Arnold Stein, whose accounts of "surprise endings" and "final twists" lend support to the Herbert she goes on to describe; and had she felt the need of it, additional support would have been available in much of the criticism produced in the past twenty years. Even Rosemond Tuve, who emphasizes what is familiar and traditional in Herbert's art, remarks that "his Jordans never stayed crossed."[6] For Tuve, the restlessness in Herbert's poetry reflects his "agony of spirit" (p. 197). Robert Montgomery offers a more formal explanation. He argues that in many poems Herbert establishes "a fictional context" the effect of which is to "remove the discourse from the level of meditation to the level of drama."[7] The "symbolic images" documented and explicated by Tuve and others function in the action of a "fable" and what is significant is what happens "within the mind and soul of the speaker" (p. 463). What happens, according to Valerie Carnes, is a

5. "The Re-invented Poem: George Herbert's Alternatives," in *Forms of Lyric*, ed. Reuben Brower (New York, 1970), p. 19.

6. *A Reading of George Herbert* (Chicago, 1952), p. 196.

7. "The Province of Allegory in George Herbert's Verse," *Texas Studies in Language and Literature*, I (1960), 461, 462.

succession of "vacillations" and "alternations," "psychological shiftings" which reflect "the 'double motion' of
the soul that yearns simultaneously for heaven and
earth."[8] The result is a poetry in which understandings
are continually being revised as "the poet's symbolic
consciousness is . . . turned back upon itself with highly
ironic effect" (p. 519). This is very close to what Vendler
intends by her phrase the "re-invented poem." Herbert
"is constantly criticising what he has already written
down, and finding the original conception inadequate"
(p. 24); "at any moment a poem by Herbert can repudiate
itself, correct itself, rephrase itself, rethink its experience,
re-invent its topic" (p. 45). For Coburn Freer, this rethink-
ing or correcting is one manifestation of what he calls
"tentative form," the result of a "discrepancy between
the way a Herbert poem behaves and the way it says it
behaves."[9] The form of a poem, Freer asserts, often argues with its "literal meaning" and the argument is
reflected in an alternation between confident assertion
and "bathetic falterings" (p. 213).

For these critics, then, the instability of Herbert's
poetry is its distinguishing characteristic, and it would
seem that what we have here is a genuine revolution in
critical attitudes, a revolution so successful that it has
literally replaced one Herbert with another. Like all rev-
olutions, however, it has produced a counter-reaction
of which Louis Martz is one of the more recent spokes-
men. "I think," observes Martz, that

we do not do Herbert's poetry a favour when we seek to emphasize its restlessness. What we have in his poetry . . . is the

8. "The Unity of George Herbert's *The Temple:* A Reconsideration,"
ELH, 35 (1968), 517.
9. *Music for A King* (Baltimore, 1972), p. 194.

memory of states of restlessness now securely overcome, and retrospectively viewed as dangers overpassed. As Herbert's *Temple* now exists it is an edifice in which the praise of God is securely rendered, from a vantage point of victory.[10]

As one might almost predict, these remarks are introduced by a comparison between "Donne's instability and Herbert's deeply achieved security," but it would be an oversimplification to conclude that Martz is simply returning to the more comfortable view of an older critical position. Rather, he is playing out his part in a sequence that will be repeated endlessly so long as critics restrict themselves to the two positions made available by the controversy. The situation is an all too familiar one in literary studies: lines of battle drawn in such a way as to create a dialectic that should *itself* be the object of interpretation. Rather than swinging back and forth between the poet of order and stability and the poet of change and surprise, Herbert criticism should ask the question posed by its own shape and history: how is it that a poet and the poetry he writes can be restless and secure *at the same time?*

Even when that question is asked, it is answered by devising strategies that displace rather than confront it. One such strategy is to create categories for the classification and analysis of different kinds of poems—"orchestral form" as opposed to "tentative form" (Freer), the "meditative" mode as opposed to the mode of allegory or fiction (Montgomery)—but while these distinctions acknowledge the two Herberts, their real service is to keep them separate and to prevent the surfacing of the

10. "The Action of the Self: Devotional Poetry in the Seventeenth Century," in *Metaphysical Poetry, Stratford-Upon-Avon Studies 11*, ed. Malcolm Bradbury and David Palmer (New York, 1970), p. 108.

issues their meeting would raise. Another strategy is implicit in Martz's emphasis on the word "memory": "What we have in his poetry is the *memory* of states of restlessness now securely overcome." Martz does not deny the restlessness (any more than the partisans of restlessness absolutely deny the security); he merely deprives it of its immediacy (and therefore of its reality) by placing it in the past. Herbert becomes his own persona, taking positions he no longer holds, and striking stances that do not reflect his present attitudes or beliefs.[11] It is only a short step from this to a third strategy, one in which the poet disappears altogether except as the craftsman of a series of dramatic monologues, complete with "fictional contexts" and a variety of fallible speakers.[12]

Actually, the second and third strategies are basically one, for they both accommodate what is tentative and provisional in Herbert's poetry by attributing it to design; and by attributing it to design (in the name of art) they take away its legitimacy, make it a trick, something that has been staged. This may seem a harsh description of what in other contexts is praised as the art that hides art, but if we are to take Herbert seriously (and that, of course, is finally the issue) it is a praise he would not have wished to receive, at least not in the context of what Tuve has characterized as a "lifelong attempt to make *of literary*

11. In a sense, then, the poetry becomes a spiritual autobiography, and it is as such that it is characterized by W. H. Halewood in *The Poetry of Grace* (New Haven, 1970), pp. 102–103.

12. Indeed, Martz has already taken that step when he urges us to "notice that the troublesome conscience is treated as a dramatic character quite distinct from the speaker's whole self" (p. 112). For another version of the "two Herberts" see Douglas Bush, *English Literature in the Earlier Seventeenth Century* (Oxford, 1945), p. 138.

creation—*entire*—a devoted and self-forgetful religious act" (p. 195).

It is here that we run up against the limits of formalism, its inability to accommodate change as a genuine (that is independent) value. This is not to say that formalist critics cannot talk about change, but they can talk about it only as the property of a formal structure, and to talk about it in that way is to make it disappear. That is, if a poem is regarded as the unified realization of a single (and therefore stable) intention, then any changes in attitude or point of view can only be seen as the product of pre-planning, and are therefore not real changes at all. (If there is a change of mind, it can only be a character's in which case it is literally a fiction.) On the other side, change can only be given legitimacy by denying the reality of planning, that is, by asserting the absence of design. This is what Vendler seems to be doing when she argues that *The Temple* is the actual (in the sense of unedited) record of a spiritual experience, one in which Herbert in midflight "suddenly reflects" (p.20), "catches himself in careless speech" (p. 21), "pulls himself up sharply from his clichés" (p. 21), "changes his mind at the last moment," constantly criticizes "what he has already written down," as, with "a remarkable lack of censorship," that is, of conscious art, he does his revising "in public" (pp. 35, 22). Vendler is herself uneasy with these formulations, and she repeatedly qualifies them with quotation marks around words like "written" and with phrases like "as it were." The suggestion is that her statements are not meant naively and that the effects she describes in the vocabulary of spontaneity ("rethinkings," "reinventions," sudden changes of mind) are, in fact, artful and planned; but this, of course, would place her in the formalist camp with all the others and leave the surprise in Herbert's poetry without even one genuine champion.

Underlying the debate over how to characterize Herbert's poetry is the familiar opposition between art and sincerity.[13] If Herbert is a craftsman, he cannot mean what he is saying because the changes he reports cannot really be occurring (they are faked, or staged, or recollected in tranquility); and if he means what he says, he isn't functioning as a craftsman because the changes are simply reported as they occur (he is a transcriber or tape-recorder). To be sure, this polarized view of Herbert criticism does not do justice to the subtlety of its practitioners, who remain agile even within the confines they have (often inadvertently) accepted, but it does do justice, I believe, to the range of possibilities that are logically available, given those confines. These possibilities are reflected at every level of the critical enterprise: in arguments over the interpretation of individual poems, in the contrasting characterizations of Herbert's religious sensibility, and, finally, in the answers given to the question that has been debated more than any other: what is the structure of *The Temple*? The range of these answers should not surprise us. At one extreme, we have attempts to tie the sections of *The Temple*—"Church-porch," "Church," "Church Militant"—and the order of the poems within them, to a pre-existing model—to the Temple of Solomon, whose architectural divisions (also threefold) were so often the object of typological interpre-

13. On this point see H. R. Swardson, *Poetry and the Fountain of Light* (Columbia, Mo., 1962), p. 81: "Herbert's poetry does reflect intensely one aspect of the tension between the Christian tradition and the classical literary tradition: the opposition between spiritual sincerity and skill in poetry, or, more crudely, between simple truth and contrived art."

tation,[14] to the plan of an Anglican Church (an interpretation implicit in Christopher Harvey's admiring imitation), to a classical temple (not so much as a model, but as a type that has been superseded),[15] to the liturgical year, to the life of the typical Christian as he moves through that year,[16] to the tripartite structure of formal (in this case Salesian) meditation,[17] and to the dramatic or psychological structure displayed by many volumes of courtly love.[18] Each of these suggestions is supported by persuasive evidence, both in the poems themselves and in the historical materials cited as their probable sources, and each of them has been challenged by an equally persuasive counter-argument. The meditative paradigm has been rejected as a model because *The Temple* does not rise to a "plateau of assurance": "the last poems of the book show very little more assurance than the earlier ones";[19] fault has been found with the analogy to the Hebraic temple because it is difficult to maintain the identification of the "holy of holies" (the inner sanctuary) with the pessimistic chronicle that is "The Church Militant";[20] the plan of an Anglican or any other Church has been opposed as an ordering principle because there are no

14. John David Walker, "The Architectonics of George Herbert's *The Temple*," *ELH*, 29 (1962), 289–305.

15. Mary Ellen Rickey, *Utmost Art* (Lexington, 1966), pp. 9–15.

16. White, *Metaphysical Poets*.

17. Louis Martz, *The Poetry of Meditation* (New Haven, 1954), pp. 147–148.

18. Elizabeth Stambler, "The Unity of Herbert's 'Temple,' " *Cross-Currents*, 13 (Summer, 1960), 251–266.

19. *Ibid.*, p. 253.

20. See Annabel M. Endicott, "The Structure of George Herbert's *Temple*: A Reconsideration," *UTQ*, 34 (1965), 226–237; and Lee Ann Johnson, "The Relationship of 'The Church Militant' to *The Temple*," *SP*, 67 (April, 1971), 200–206.

matching correspondences in the order of the poems: in Herbert's Church the first piece of furniture one encounters is the altar, but as Mary Rickey points out, "In no Christian Church . . . does one find this fixture immediately inside the entrance, and upon reading the 'Superliminare' one has figuratively gone through the door" (pp. 9–10).

Predictably, the failure of these models to explain every aspect of *The Temple* has led some to argue that the sequence of the poems is random. This randomness has been praised as evidence of "Herbert's psychological realism," of his intention to reproduce in poetry the violent fluctuations of the spiritual life,[21] and it has been excused as the result of an intention either abandoned or left unfulfilled.[22] Support for the second of these positions has been found in the doubtful status of "The Church Militant" (in the manuscripts there are blank pages between it and the end of "The Church")[23] and in the possibility that "The Temple" may not even be Herbert's title.[24] The inconclusiveness of the evidence on either side of these questions has the effect of leaving the critic to his own devices: he may either ignore the complex of problems entirely and concentrate on the explication of individual poems, or, proceeding on the assumption that the work is unfinished, he may propose, as did George Herbert Palmer, to perfect or complete it, in ac-

21. Joseph Summers, *George Herbert: His Religion and Art* (Cambridge, Mass., 1954), p. 87.

22. White, *Metaphysical Poets,* p. 162.

23. See *The Works of George Herbert,* ed. F. E. Hutchinson (Oxford, 1941), p. liii. All references to Herbert's poetry are to this edition.

24. On this point, see J. Max Patrick, "Critical Problems in Editing George Herbert's *The Temple,"* in *The Editor As Critic and The Critic As Editor,* ed. Murray Krieger (Los Angeles, 1973), pp. 3–40.

cord, of course, with what must have been, or should have been, Herbert's intention.

It is not *my* intention to join this debate, but to point out how it is one more manifestation of the dialectic that is the content of Herbert criticism at every level, whether the issue is the characterization of the poetry, or the quality of the poet's faith, or the significance of his divisions and titles. It is a dialectic of choice, and the choice is always between a structure that is firm, secure, and complete, and a structure (if structure is the word) that is precarious, shifting, and unfinished. Insofar as these choices are perceived as mutually exclusive, the dialectic is self-perpetuating; for in order to maintain one position, it is necessary to ignore or de-emphasize evidence for the other; and sooner or later that evidence will be the basis for a "reassessment" and the occasion for beginning the sequence again. It follows, then, that rather than perpetuating the dialectic, a way must be found of escaping it, of breaking out of the prison the criticism has fashioned for itself so that we may confront directly the question implicit in its alternations: how is it that the same body of poetry has been the basis for reaching contradictory, but equally persuasive, interpretive conclusions? The thesis of the following pages is that the answer to this question will be found in the forms, concerns, and conventions of the Reformation catechism.

2. ROTE AND SOCRATEAN CATECHIZING

Herbert's interest in catechistical theory and practice is easily documented, and by 1670, it is a part of his legend. Of the three "Salisbury walks" reported by Walton, two involve catechizing directly or indirectly. On one occasion, Herbert overtakes a gentleman from Salisbury, and with very little preface, asks from him "some account of his faith."[25] The request is not casual; it is an allusion to I Peter 3:15—"be ready always to give an answer to every man that asketh you a reason of the hope that is in you"—the text most often cited in support of the "necessity and profit" of catechizing and one that appears on the title pages of many Reformation catechisms. It is certainly cue enough for this gentleman, who readily responds to Herbert's "needful questions," and is afterwards given "rules for the tryal of his sincerity" (p. 61), that is, rules for the practice of self-catechizing. On another occasion, Walton tells us, Herbert meets with a "neighbor minister" and their talk turns to possible cures for the wickedness of the times. Herbert proposes three: the keeping of Ember-weeks more strictly, the practicing by clergymen of what they preach ("For this would force a love and imitation, and an unfeigned reverence from all that knew them to be such"), and the restoring of *"the great and neglected duty of Catechizing, on which the salvation of so many of the poor and ignorant lay-people does depend"* (p. 62).[26]

Neither of these incidents bears the stamp of a unique and individual experience, and they may well be instances of Walton's tendency to hagiography. More reliable evidence of a connection between Herbert and catechizing comes from Barnabas Oley and John Ferrar,

25. Izaak Walton, *The Lives of Dr. John Donne, Sir Henry Wotton, Mr. Richard Hooker, Mr. George Herbert* (1670), p. 60.

26. In *A Light from Christ, Leading unto Christ, by the star of his word* (1646), Immanuel Bourne asserts that "a principal cause" of ignorance "was and is want of Catechizing" (sig. A6ᵛ). Evidently, the complaint was a common one in the literature.

the biographer of his brother Nicholas. While traveling in Italy, Nicholas had come across a catechistical manual written by Ludovicus Carbo, and had undertaken to translate it, in order to *"stir up us Ministers to be painfull in that excellent labour of the Lord*, catechizing."[27] It was Ferrar's practice, as his brother reports, to make Herbert "the Peruser . . . of what he did as in those three Translations of Valdezzo, Lessius, & Carbo. To the first Mr. Herbert made an Epistle, To the second, he sent to add that of Cornarius Temperance, & well approved of the last."[28] This translation has apparently not survived (it was denied publication, although Maycock, Ferrar's biographer, claims that it was published in 1636),[29] but this description of it was found in the papers of a Mr. John Mapleton: "Of the instruction of children in the Christian doctrine, by Ludovico Carbone, 1636. Wherein is demonstrated how necessary, worthy and acceptable to God this exercise of teaching the Christian doctrine is, and what profit children, masters, private families, cities and the whole Church reaps thereby."[30]

We are not in a position to say what it is that Herbert "well approved" in Carbo's manual, but it is safe to assume that he would have liked the emphasis on the importance of catechizing not only for children, but for "masters, private families, cities and the whole Church." This larger view is typical of Reformation theorists (which may be the reason for Oley's characterization of

27. Barnabas Oley, *Herbert's Remains* (1652), sig. b1ᵛ.

28. *The Ferrar Papers*, ed. B. Blackstone (Cambridge, 1938), p. 509.

29. A. L. Maycock, *Nicholas Ferrar of Little Gidding* (London, 1938), p. 272.

30. *Nicholas Ferrar: Two Lives By His Brother John And By Doctor Jebb* (Cambridge, 1855), p. 302.

Carbo's book as "that Egyptian Jewell") and it is very much reflected in Herbert's own treatise *A Priest To the Temple, Or The Countrey Parson His Character And Rule of Holy Life*. References to catechizing appear often in this volume, in the injunction to the parson to order his life "that when death takes him . . . he may say as He did, *I sate daily with you teaching in the Temple*" (pp. 227–228), in the chapter on *The Parsons Accessary Knowledges* (p. 230), in the citing of I Cor. 14, *"Let all things be done to edification"* as one of the apostle's two great rules (p. 246), in the account of the Parson's duties when in circuit (p. 248), and in the description of what he does to prepare his flock for the receiving of the sacraments (pp. 258–259). Each of these contexts is significant for the argument I shall be presenting, but they are all subsidiary to the *theoretical* context established in Chapter xxi, *The Parson Catechising*.

Much of what Herbert says in this chapter is thoroughly commonplace. The parson catechizes in order "to infuse a competent knowledge of salvation in every one of his Flock" (p. 255). This is but one of the "three points of his duty" (the other two being building up this knowledge and making it the basis of a "reformation of life"), yet it is fundamental because without it, the others "cannot be attained." "Every one of his flock" includes not only children, but their parents and masters, all of whom are required to be present at the catechizing of their charges in addition to receiving catechistical instruction themselves.[31] The mode of instruction will differ with the age and degree of "growth" of the individual. From the "younger sort," the parson will exact

31. Compare Samuel Crooke, *The guide unto true blessednesse*, sixth edition (1640), sig. A6^r. "The spirit both of the answerer, and of all that attend, is stirred up to bethinke themselves what might be most aptly answered, to the question propounded."

"the very words" of the ordinary catechism, that is, of the catechism as it appears in the Book of Common Prayer (1604); older parishioners (who are to be questioned in private, as befits their age) will be asked to go beyond the words and penetrate to "the substance." Lest this suggest that the goal of catechizing—the building up of knowledge—is ever fully achieved, Herbert emphasizes that even those who are "well grown in the knowledge of Religion" should seize every possible occasion to "examine their grounds, renew their vowes, and . . . inlarge their meditations." The catechizing of others can provide such an occasion, not only for masters and parents, but also for the parson, who, as he discharges his duty, at the same time performs an "exercise upon himself . . . for the advancing of his own mortification." In this way, the parson will be "growing with the growth of his Parish."

It is here that Herbert begins to diverge slightly from the usual pattern followed by those who write in praise of catechizing. His emphasis on the benefits to be derived from this "admirable, and singular" work (p. 230), is conventional, but by including the catechist among the beneficiaries he sets himself apart, and suggests a view of the transaction considerably more dynamic that that held by his predecessors and contemporaries. In his preface to the English translation of Nowell's *Catechism* (the only work of its kind to be approved by the Convocation of Bishops and Clergy), Thomas Norton offers this description of the relationship between master and pupil:

It may not be thought that the master here inquireth of the scholar as desirous to learn of him, nor that the scholar informeth the master as presuming to teach him. But the master opposeth the scholar to see how he hath profited, and the scholar rendereth to the master to give accompt of his memory and diligence . . . The end and purpose of catechism is . . . to serve the good use of confirmation by the bishop, at which time the bishop which confirmeth doth not teach, but examine, and in his whole manner of opposing useth such form as here in like sort the *Catechumenus* or child is prepared unto.[32]

While Norton begins by warning against a misinterpretation that would make a teacher of the pupil, he ends by eliminating teaching (at least as Herbert would have understood it) altogether. Since the bishop does not teach, but examines, that is, tests the ability of the scholar to give set answers to set questions, the preparation for that one-time performance should observe the same form. The emphasis, then, will be on repetition and drill ("memory and diligence") and the procedure will be a success if at the end of it the student is letter perfect.

This is learning of a very limited kind. Herbert labels it correctly as "rote" and complains that it produces many who "say the Catechisme . . . without piercing into the sense of it" (p. 256). The complaint is a common one in the literature (where it is often directed at the perfunctory and mechanical practices of the papists), but even when the deficiency is acknowledged, the proposed reforms seem hardly calculated to correct it. Herbert Palmer hopes to prevent an "error observable in diverse learners, who . . . oft give the Answer, which they have learned by rote, to a wrong question, to the great confounding of their understandings."[33] In order to remedy this situation, Palmer devises a system of double checks. Not only will the learner be required to respond

32. *A Catechism Written in Latin By Alexander Nowell, Dean of St. Paul's Together with The Same Catechism Translated into English by Thomas Norton*, ed. G.E. Corrie for The Parker Society (Cambridge, 1853), p. 109.

33. *Endeavor of making the Principles of Christian Religion*, 3rd impression (1644), sig. A2[v].

in full sentences, but after each response he will be asked a series of additional questions that can only be answered "yes" or "no." Thus to the question, "Since you say that none can so perfectly repent as to be without all sin . . . how shall any man be saved?" one should give the answer, "Even those that repent have need to be saved by Jesus Christ, and his satisfaction" (p. 13). There then follow four subsidiary questions: "Can a man's own righteousnesse save him?" "Can he make satisfaction to God for his sins by them?" "*Or*, by any other means of his procuring?" "Have even those that repent, need to be saved by Jesus Christ and his Satisfaction?" The effect of such a sequence will be twofold: it will interrupt the hypnotic rhythm of the more usual form and it will confirm the learner's understanding of his answer by requiring that he give it again from another direction. It is, however, the same answer, even when it is reconfirmed by a series of yes's and no's (in this case three no's and a yes); that is, the effect has not been to eliminate rote, but to perfect it. The pupil will have substituted for the rote learning of words the rote learning of set arguments, and while the understanding will have been unconfounded in the sense that the question and answer will now go together, it will still be mechanical.

As unadventurous as he is, Palmer is nevertheless unusual for going even this far. The more typical prescription for the dangers of rote is more of the same. It is a prescription that follows inevitably given the (false) derivation of catechism from the Greek word meaning "echo."[34] The catechists who remark on this derivation (and they are many) almost always end by extrapolating

34. See on this point, M. Rieu, *Catechetics* (Chicago, 1927), p. 3, and Crooke, *The guide,* sig. B2ᵛ.

from it a methodology. Thus, after explaining that "the name of catechizing . . . hath his original from a Greeke word that signifies to *sound* or *resound* as by an echo," Samuel Crooke finds a parallel in "Moses injoyning this duty . . . *for thou shalt repeat these words* (saith hee) *unto thy children.*"[35] "What is it," Crooke asks, "to *repeat* them, but to make them as it were a *proverbe* in every one's mouth . . . that they may the better fasten both on . . . memory & conscience?" (sigs. B2ᵛ–B3ʳ). From this rhetorical query, it is an easy step to Crooke's endorsing of the question and answer form of catechizing because it is so well suited to the limited goals of drill and repetition: "the heads and grounds of religion being by this meanes inculcated, are the more likely by continuall sounding in the eare, to take rooting in the memory, and ever to sinke and settle in the minde" (sig. B5ᵛ). It is "this meanes" that Crooke later opposes to speaking "some good words as rote" (sig. B7ʳ). His distinction, like Palmer's, is between a learning that is random (*some* good words) and a learning that is systematic, between a parrot-like recital of fragments and a comprehending recital of whole sentences and even of set arguments. The distinction is a real one, but insofar as the procedure is designed largely to improve memory, the advance in understanding will be minimal.

The commitment of the catechists to memorization, and therefore to drill and repetition, is reflected in their metaphors. "The duty of the catechized," says Lancelot Andrewes, is "to goe over the same matter, as the knife doth the whetstone, and to repeat it till they have made it their owne."[36] Robert Allen compares catechizing to "the

---

35. *The guide,* sig. B1ᵛ.
36. *A patterne of catechisticall doctrine* (1630), pp. 8–9.

making of an impression by a stamp or seale."[37] For Crooke, the catechistical precepts are *"grafts* of grace" which one is "to insert into the crab-stockes of nature" (sig. B6r). It is necessary, he says, "to strike them to and fro upon the eare & tongue of the childe, that they may the better fasten both on his memory & conscience" (sig. B3r). "So needful a thing it is in all religions," declares William Charcke, "often to beate in the first groundes."[38] "Fathers," Jeremias Bastingius advises, "should summarily beat into their children the chief points of the Law" (*An exposition or commentarie upon the catechisme*, 1589, sig. A3r).

While the metaphors vary, the picture they project is consistent: the catechist labors long and hard to work alterations in materials that are at once resistant and passive, and because they are resistant and passive, the tools he employs will be blunt and crude (the whetstone, the stamp, the hammer blows of drill and repetition). As Arthur Dent points out, so mechanical a procedure can only be "irksome and tedious" and his description of it can be taken as a singularly honest account of the state of the art in the early seventeenth century:

> We must not be ashamed to use repetitions, and tautologies, and to tell them one thing, twentie times over and over againe; here a line, and there a line; here a little and there a little, precept upon precept . . . I know right well, nothing goeth more against the stomach of a scholler, and him that is learned indeed, then to doe thus.[39]

It is against this background that the uniqueness of

---

37. *A treasurie of catechisme, or christian instruction* (1600), p. 2.

38. *Of the use of catechising* (1580), sig. D3r.

39. *The plaine mans path-way to Heaven* (1603), p. 332. See also Augustine, *De Catechizandis Rudibus*, trans. and annot. by the Rev. Joseph P. Christopher (Westminster, Maryland, 1946), pp. 34ff.

Herbert's position emerges. Like his contemporaries, he deplores rote (those who learn by it perform "as parrats"), and at first the reforms he suggests are moderate: go over the catechism, but "in other words"; keep the order of the larger divisions (creed, commandments, lord's prayer, sacraments), but within them, vary the order of the questions. These techniques are like Palmer's in that they seem designed to prevent the pupil from making too automatic (and therefore uncomprehending) an association between question and answer. Herbert, however, does not stop here: he goes on to advise that this varying of the order should itself be varied according to the capacity of the individual.[40] ("This order being used to one, would be a little varyed to another.") Even this could be read in the light of the conventional distinction between the catechizing of children and the catechizing of the "elder sort" were it not for the following sentence:

And this is an admirable way of teaching, wherein the Catechized will at length finde delight, and by which the Catechizer, if he once get the skill of it, will draw out of ignorant and silly souls, even the dark and deep points of Religion. (p. 256)

Two things about this statement strike one immediately: it attributes "delight" to an experience that is, by almost any other account, painful, and it grants to the catechized full partnership in the transaction. Rather than being worked on (stamped, carved, ground, filled) as if he were an inert piece of wax or wood or metal, he is working, cooperating in the process of his own "drawing out"

40. Here Herbert's likely source is Augustine. See below, Chapter Four, section 1.

(that is, his education), a descriptive phrase that implies there is already in him something to be drawn. He is not an empty vessel waiting to be filled. The "delight" that he then experiences is the delight of self-discovery, in the double sense of discovering something about himself (the knowledge he sought was already, in part, his) and of making the discovery himself (with of course the aid of the catechizer). Both these senses are captured in Herbert's praise of the catechism so conducted: "the secret of whose good consists in this . . . when one is asked a question, he must discover what he is" (p. 257).[41] Clearly this is not a question for which there is a rote or set answer, but one whose purpose it is to set the listener's mind to working. There is a word or name for this kind of questioning, and Herbert acknowledges it in his very next sentence:

Socrates did thus in Philosophy, who held that the seeds of all truth lay in every body, and accordingly by questions well ordered he found Philosophy in silly Trades-men.

---

41. Herbert likes this phrase so much that he repeats it in the next chapter. It has been pointed out to me that the phrase can be construed to mean that the asking of a question, as opposed to the delivering of a sermon, will reveal whether or not a parishioner has been paying attention. That is, "he must discover what he is" could mean only that he will have to show himself as either having been awake or asleep. There seems to me to be evidence in the passage for both readings. The narrower reading is suggested by the comparison between catechizing and preaching ("at Sermons, and Prayers, men may sleep or wander") while the larger reading is appropriate in the context of the emphasis throughout on Socratic techniques for involving and drawing out an interlocutor. At any rate, there is no need to choose between the two readings, because they support rather than exclude one another: it is in being kept awake in one sense that the Answerer will be led to become awake in a more spiritual sense, discovering what he is by repeatedly revealing where he is.

Herbert is quick to point out that Socrates cannot serve as
a perfect type of the catechist, because his "position will
not hold in Christianity," which "contains things above
nature." That is to say, the philosopher's success in
drawing from a slave boy the laws of geometry cannot be
paralleled by the Christian pedagogue, since the law he
teaches—the law of faith—is unavailable to merely
natural capacities; it must be *revealed*. For Crooke this
distinction is enough to disqualify the pagan
philosophers as catechistical models; they deal only in
vain wisdom and "lack . . . the wisdom of God."[42] Herbert, however, not only pronounces the dialogues of
Plato "worth the reading," but urges that the "singular
dexterity of Socrates . . . be . . . imitated." He thus sets
himself apart from the Protestant tradition, in which, as
one authority notes, catechistical instruction is specif-
ically "not Socratic, i.e. does not aim to draw out what is
in the mind of the pupil."[43] On those rare occasions
when other theorists cite Socrates, they do so only to
point out that he too uses the question and answer
method;[44] any "imitation," however, does not extend to
the *heuristics* of that method, for as M. Rieu observes, by
"questions" those catechists who follow Luther mean
"examination questions or confessional questions, not
developing questions."[45]

Herbert, on the other hand, obviously means developing questions, and in his extended description of the par-

42. *The guide,* sig. B8^v.

43. *Cyclopedia of Biblical, Theological, and Ecclesiastical Literature* (New
York, 1868), p. 149.

44. See John Poynet, *Catechismus brevis christianae disciplinae summam
continens* (1553), sig. Aiiii^r; Crooke, *The guide,* sig. B6^r.

45. *Catechetics,* p. 114.

son's practice "in this kind," the "skill" is said to consist "but in these three points":

First, an aim and mark of the whole discourse, whither to drive the Answerer, which the Questionist must have in his mind before any question be propounded, upon which and to which the questions are to be chained. Secondly, a most plain and easie framing the question, even containing in vertue the answer also, especially to the more ignorant. Thirdly, when the answerer sticks, an illustrating the thing by something else, which he knows, making what hee knows to serve him in that which he knows not. (pp. 256–257)

Again, this is a mixture of traditional and innovative advice. The chaining of the questions is a feature of many catechisms. A sequence from John Ball's *Short questions and answers explaining the common catechisme* (1639) will serve as an illustration:

Q. *Can you perfectly fulfill all these Commandments?*
A. No, I am not able to fulfill any one of them, in any one duty, according to that exact perfection it requires.
Q. *What punishment deserve you by the breach of them?*
A. Eternall destruction both of body and soule, which is due to everyone that breaketh any of these lawes, in the least duty required in it.
Q. *How may one escape that punishment?*
A. By laying hold on Christ by Faith, who endured the full punishment of sinne in his body on the crosse, for all that truly repent of their sinnes.
Q. *What is repentance?* (sigs. B6^r–B6^v)

One can easily see this chain stretching on and on, but its links would be formal and internal; that is, they would depend on the (theological) logic of the point under discussion, a logic to which both the Questionist and Answerer would be prebound. In Herbert's formulation, however, the logic of chaining is rhetorical; it is tied not to the structure of doctrine (although doctrine is the material with which it works) but to the structure of the situation, and its goal is not the orderly disposition of a body of knowledge, but the arrival at that knowledge of a respondent who has come to it himself. In other words, the "well ordered" in Herbert's well-ordered questions refers to a *strategy* rather than to a pre-existing order. The goal of the strategy is the self-discovery of the respondent, and in the service of that goal the catechist will employ any and all the techniques that make "some dialogues in *Plato* . . . worth the reading": he will pose deliberately naive questions ("even containing in vertue the answer also"); he will take positions, not because he holds them, but in the hope that they will draw a corrective or completing response ("making what hee knows serve him in that which he knows not"); he will, in short, do anything to "drive the Answerer" to the mark that has all the while been "in his mind."

The distance between this and the cut and dried transaction described by other catechists could hardly be greater. When catechizing is regarded as a strategy rather than as an examination, the relationship between the respective parties changes radically. In an examination, everyone's cards are out on the table: the roles to be played are well and narrowly defined, and they are fully understood by the participants, each of whom is aware of what will count as a successful performance. Moreover, those performances, if they are forthcoming, will cooperate in completing a specific program; and that program, at least in its general shape and often in its every detail, will have been known and agreed to in advance.(That is why students feel justified in complaining if an examination includes a "surprise" question.) In the executing of a strategy, however, the program will be known to only one of the parties; the other must grope toward a knowledge that will completely escape him until he stumbles upon it. It follows, then, that the moment of stumbling, of dawning realization, will always be a surprise (as it must be, if it is to constitute a *self*-discovery), and yet at the same time it will always have been contrived. In other words, the situation is at once both structured and open: the structure belongs to the catechist whose questions will be the ordered product of his intention, the intention to drive the Answerer to one of the "dark and deep points of Religion"; the openness belongs to the Answerer who will at first see neither that point nor the point of what will appear to him to be a succession of unrelated questions. As Herbert observes in Chapter XXII *(The Parson in Sacraments)* the goal of self-discovery will be achieved only if the questions are propounded "loosely and wildely" (p. 259), for only then will the respondent experience the "delight" of working things out for himself; but what is loose and wild from his perspective will have been carefully planned from the perspective of the catechist, who will experience "delight" of quite a different kind, the delight of having produced, that is, *designed*, spontaneity; not, however, in himself, but in another.

3. DRIVING TO THE MARK: THE SHAPE OF CATECHISTICAL POETRY

It is no accident, I believe, that we need only alter this formula slightly and it will serve very nicely as a way of accounting for the simultaneous presence in Herbert's poetry of order and surprise. One need only replace the catechist and his pupil with the poet and his reader. To the one belongs the stability of a prior and controlling intention, and to the other belongs the realization of that intention, a realization which, because it is in the nature of a self-discovery, will be preceded by uncertainty and restlessness, and crowned by surprise. Moreover that surprise will be real, even though it will have been staged. Order and unpredictability can both be given legitimacy because they have been divided between the poet and his reader, and a critic is not constrained to choose between de-emphasizing the one or domesticating the other. This choice, as we have seen, arises because the intuitions underlying it—that the poetry is stable and that the poetry is restless—cannot be accommodated within a formalist perspective without entailing a contradiction. The contradiction disappears, however, if the two intuitions are parceled out; that is, if they are not assumed to be the exclusive property either of a formal structure or of a single personality, but of a *situation*. Herbert's theory of catechizing provides a way of doing just that, and thus makes it possible to acknowledge both his art and his sincerity without compromising either. Indeed they become interdependent: rather than being a sincere report of a mind in the act of changing, the poem is a sincere effort on the part of the poet-catechist to change his reader-pupil's mind. Sincerity is thus not a bodiless interior phenomenon in relation to which a poem is merely a transcription; sincerity is inseparable from an intention in relation to which a poem (or some other act) is an implementation. In the catechistical situation, the intention is to drive the pupil to a deep and dark point of religion, and its sincere implementation involves the catechist in any number of artful practices (he is a sincere role-player[46]), including indirection and even, if the occasion demands, deception.

What I am suggesting then is that Herbert's poetry is a strategy, and that as a strategy it shares with the catechistical practice of his parson a shape and a goal: the goal is the involvement of the reader in his own edification (a word, as we shall see, that is precisely intended) and the shape is the bringing of the reader "by questions well ordered" to "that which he knows not." This is not to say that the poetry is in the form of questions (although it sometimes is),[47] but that it functions as questions function, by drawing from the reader a completing, or correcting, or, in some cases, a mistaken, response. That response is given not simply at the end of the poem, but at every moment in it; it is a developing response, and its development is the true drama of this poetry, even when a poem is itself dramatic in form. Consider, as an example, the poem "Love-joy":

> As on a window late I cast mine eye,
> I saw a vine drop grapes with *J* and *C*
> Anneal'd on every bunch. One standing by
> Ask'd what it meant. I, who am never loth
> To spend my judgement, said, It seem'd to me
> To be the bodie and the letters both
> Of *Joy* and *Charitie*. Sir, you have not miss'd,
> The man reply'd; It figures *JESUS CHRIST*.

Robert Montgomery has described "Love-joy" as a "brief compressed narrative," "a presentation of and commentary upon the imperfection of one man's understanding of Christian truth." The imperfection is the narrator's and it is revealed by "the order of the two interpreta-

46. I owe this characterization to Donald Friedman.
47. See, for example, "Businesse."

tions," the second of which "gently contradicts his judgement" (p. 462). In the course of the poem, however, it is not the narrator's but the reader's judgment that is contradicted, at least temporarily. Even before the poem's official questioner ("One standing by") appears in line 3, his question is being asked by the hieroglyphic riddle of lines 1 and 2: what do J and C annealed on a bunch of grapes signify? The obvious answer is, of course, Jesus Christ, and it is the answer the reader will be ready to deliver and is expecting to hear, especially since the word "bodie" would seem to allude directly to the typological association of the bunch of grapes in Numbers (13:23–33) with the wine press of the Passion.[48] Thus for most of the poem it is the reader who is spending his judgment (the figure in the poem has not yet hazarded anything), and it is with some surprise that he hears the speaker give what is apparently the wrong answer: "It seem'd to me / To be the bodie and the letters both / Of Joy and Charitie." This, however, is only the first of three surprises. The second occurs when the narrator's answer is approved by the Questionist ("Sir, you have not miss'd"), for then it seems that the reader has spent his judgment unwisely; but when the answer is expanded and completed (this is the third surprise), it turns out to be exactly what he had been expecting after all: "It figures JESUS CHRIST." Rather than gently contradicting the judgment of the speaker, the "order of the two interpretations" confirms the (initial) judgment of the reader, but only after it had appeared that he would have to choose between them, that the answer to the poem's riddle would be *either* Jesus Christ or Joy and

48. See Tuve, *A Reading*, pp. 112–123.

Charitie. The revelation that it is both does not merely reassure the reader, but asks him to re-examine his own position, not because it has been (finally) challenged, but because it has been shown to include more than even he knew; has been shown to include Joy and Charitie. Montgomery concludes that one answer (the second) is more complete than the other, but the point is, rather, that properly understood, they imply each other. It is that understanding to which the reader is directed by the method of "questions well ordered," questions which bring him to the *self*-discovery that is the goal of the parson's catechizing. Like the parishioner in Herbert's description, the reader has been brought by means "of what he knows"—that J and C stand for Jesus Christ—to "that which he knows not"—that truly to know Jesus Christ is also to know joy and charity.

The relevance of catechizing to a reading of "Love-joy" has been asserted before, by the very first of Herbert's commentators, George Ryley. In his *Mr. Herbert's Temple and Church Militant Explained and Improved by a Discourse Upon Each Poem Critical and Practical* (1714–1715), Ryley asks us to take notice of the one who "Ask'd what it meant": "Observe," he says, "the question is Ask't by him, that Understood the Sence, in order to help the Examinant, if there was occasion."[49] If we substitute "Answerer" for Ryley's "Examinant," the parallel with Herbert's formulation in a *Priest To the Temple* is exact: the one that understands the sense has the "aim and mark of

49. *Mr. Herbert's Temple and Church Militant Explained and Improved by a Discourse Upon Each Poem Critical and Practical by George Ryley: A Critical Edition*, ed. J. M. Heissler, Diss. University of Illinois (1960), p. 379. Hereafter this text will be cited as Heissler, followed by the appropriate page number.

the whole discourse in his mind . . . before any question be propounded," a mark and aim to which the Examinant-Answerer is helped by the occasion. Ryley uses the occasion of his own commentary to point a lesson for the reader:

Private Christians would do well to Endeavor one Another's Instruction, & Improvement. And if we were Less Shy of Exposing our own weakness we might become better proficient in Christian knowledge. It's good maxim in y^e *School—qui mihi;* thus Translated.

> Resolve y^r Reading often in y^r Mind;
> Doubt as you Read. It is ye way to find.

This couplet precisely anticipates the direction in which I would extend Ryley's observations; he points out that the poem presents a catechistical situation and I would add that it also initiates one, insofar as it is the reader who is moved by the poem to expose his weakness so that he "might become better proficient in Christian knowledge." That proficiency is curious just in the measure that the knowledge is Christian; for its achievement is marked not by the acquisition of new information, but by a deeper understanding of information the learner has long possessed. That is to say, the distance between what the reader knows and "that which he knows not" is, in the way we usually measure these things, very small.

It is even smaller in "Jesu," a poem that is at once simpler and more difficult than "Love-joy"; simpler because the answer to its question is given twice (in the title and the first word) even before it begins, and more difficult because the answer to its question is given twice even before it begins; for that raises another question, not of what is going on, but of why *anything* is going on, since in the first line and one half everything seems to be already settled:

> Jesu is in my heart, his sacred name
> Is deeply carved there.

This is the kind of statement or realization with which other Herbert poems conclude (see, for example, "Jordan II"). It is an obvious reference to II Corinthians 3:2–5, a passage that begins by declaring "Ye are our epistle, written in our hearts" and ends with the admission that "our sufficiency is of God." The adverb "deeply" is read as a claim by the speaker that his happy state is stable. This stability is upset, however, by the very next word:

> but th' other week
> A great affliction broke the little frame,
> Ev'n all to pieces: which I went to seek.

This shift into the past tense retroactively complicates our sense of the present in line 1. It now seems that rather than referring to a continual state (Jesu is always in my heart), it refers to a state recovered after a time when it was lost (Jesu is now once again in my heart). This leads to the expectation that in what remains of the poem the history of that recovery will be recounted; just as the speaker sets out at the end of line 4 to seek the pieces of his "little frame," so is the reader seeking the details of his success, and, in the lines that follow, both seekings are rewarded with a disconcerting ease:

> And first I found the corner, where was *J*,
> After, where *E S*, and next where *U* was graved.

For a second time, everything is neatly settled. It would seem that the poem is over and that it was trivial. All that is left is for the speaker to put together the letters he has found. The reader, of course, already knows what they spell; and he is as confident in his knowledge (it is deeply carved) as the speaker was before his great affliction.

That confidence, however, is proved premature by a conclusion he had not anticipated:

> When I had got these parcels, instantly
> I sat me down to spell them, and perceived
> That to my broken heart he was *I ease you*,
>   And to my whole is *JESU*.

The mechanism by which Herbert brings us to the surprise of the penultimate line has been explained first by Ryley and then by Hutchinson:

This poem is an Ingenious turn of tho't upon ye Name of our Saviour. The Greeks had no J Consonant; therefore in y^t Language it has 3 syllables . . . i e s u. Thus, breaking the first syllable into two, It stands in partly [*sic*] of Sound, like *I ease you*. (p. 365)

The differentiation of I and J, whether in manuscript or in print, was not complete in Herbert's time. . . . In *B* the same capital letter is used for the consonant as for the vowel, but *1633* prints J for the last word of 1.5, the title, and the first and last words of the poem. The last word of 1.5 must be pronounced *I*, as it rhymes with *instantly*, while *Jesu* (ll. 1, 10) is a disyllable with the first letter as a consonant. (p. 516)

What Hutchinson does not see is that while the last word of line 5 must finally be pronounced as *I*, it is likely that at first it will be read as *J* because "instantly," which might determine the question, does not appear until line 7. Hutchinson himself notes that since the first word of the poem is obviously a disyllable, its initial letter would be pronounced as a consonant, in accordance with the rule delivered by Simon Daines and Thomas Lye, among countless others:

J in the beginning of a syllable preceeding another vowell always degenerates into a Consonant.
J always a con-so-nant when A Vowel follows it in the same syllabl, as *Ja*-cob *Je*-sus *Jo*-seph *Ju*-das.[50]

It follows, then, that the same letter (from, we are allowed to assume, the same word) will also be received as a consonant when it appears in the final position of line 5, and will be sounded as either "jee," as in modern "jeep," or as "yee," as in modern "yeast."[51] It is possible that this reading will be revised in line 7 so as to rhyme with "instantly," but it is equally possible that the "mistake" will persist through line 9 where it will be exposed by the revelation of *"I ease you."*

In other words, the poem is arranged so as to maximize the surprise of line 9 by inviting the reader, in lines 5 and 6, to "spell" incorrectly. The sequence is exactly like that in "Love-joy": the expectation of an apparently obvious answer, followed by the appearance of an answer neither expected nor (at first glance) obvious, but one that, in a final reversal, is placed in a pointed juxtaposition with the first:

> That to my broken heart he was *I ease you*,
> And to my whole is *JESU*.

50. *Orthoepeia Anglicana* (1640), p. 43; *The Child's Delight* (1671), p. 105. See also O.P., *Vocal Organ* (1665), p. 5.

51. On this point, see Charles Butler, *The English Grammar* (1634), p. 2; Richard Hodges, *The English Primrose* (1644), p. 9; Christopher Cooper, *The English Teacher* (1687), p. 25; Lye, *The Child's Delight*, p. 2. This argument will hold even if the letters in question were printed as "I," since in the hand-books that orthographic mark did indiscriminate duty for both sounds.

The sense of this couplet asserts a distinction that is taken away by the rhyme: for since "I ease you" is included in the *meaning* of Jesus, the difference between the heart broken and the heart whole is less significant than the rhetoric of the poem has suggested. In either case, Jesu is, in fact, in the speaker's heart, and indeed he is most palpably there when his presence registers as an easing, that is, in times of great affliction. (It is but a tuning of his breast to make the music better.)[52] It would seem, then, that we have not only "misspelled" Jesu, but misread the situation of the speaker (these two mistakes are finally one) by imitating in our experience *his* misreading (he too had failed to see the "I ease you" in Jesu). The present tense of the first line does not, after all, refer to a previous state of lost security, but to a continual present in which variations are to be seen not as departures, but as transformations. ("Whether I flie with angels, fall with dust / Thy hands made both, and I am there.")[53] The poem, then, is another of those (like "The Search," "Sepulchure," "Even-song," "Temper I") in which the search for Christ ends in the realization that he is everywhere, as he now can be found everywhere in this poem. As the first and last word of the poem, he is its frame, and he is also the frame (body) that is broken in line 3. It is because his frame is first broken and then "graved" (put into the grave) that hearts broken as his was can be eased. All of this is contained in the name Jesu, a name the reader always knew in one sense, but knows in its fullness when he is drawn into the interpretive drama the poem reports. Like those who say the

52. See "Temper I," lines 23–24.
53. "Temper I," lines 25–26.

catechism by rote, he knew the form "without piercing into the sense of it," and piercing into the sense of it is the exercise to which the poem invites him.

As formal structures "Love-joy" and "Jesu" are very different poems—in one there are two characters, in the other only the speaker is heard; in one the situation is superficially naturalistic, in the other frankly allegorical—but as strategies, they are, as we have seen, very much the same. Both work by inviting the reader to a premature interpretive conclusion, which is first challenged, and then reinstated, but in such a way as to make it the vehicle of a deeper understanding; and in both, the reader plays the role assigned in *A Priest To the Temple* to the catechized, moving by stages and in response to questions (overt or implied) to that which he knows not by means of that which he knows. My argument is that this pattern is to be found everywhere in *The Temple* and that it cuts across the distinctions one might usually make between the kinds of poems Herbert writes. In other words, the bestowing of the label "catechistical" on a Herbert poem is to a large extent independent of its structural features. What is crucial is not the dialogue in the poem, but the dialogue the poem is in, and that, in turn, is a function of the way these poems characteristically engage their readers.

In the two poems we have examined, that engagement is mediated: the reader's career develops in relation to the career of the speaker, who is also in the position of a learner. In other poems the engagement is more direct: the role of the catechized is left empty, and the reader naturally rushes in to fill it. "The Church-floore," for example, opens with a question that has the effect at once of positioning the reader, and assigning him a task:

> Mark you the floore? that square & speckled stone,
> Which looks so firm and strong,
>   Is *Patience*.

In this first stanza and the three that follow it, the reader is at once inside and outside the pedagogical situation. He is inside because it is he who is addressed, but he is outside, because the solution to the succession of emblematic riddles is handed over to him by the speaker. He does not have to work for it, and indeed working for it would have done him no good, since the meanings attached to the stones, grading, and cement of the floor are not natural, but imposed. The pause that precedes the short third line of each stanza is the equivalent of the magician's flourish just before he reveals to a wondering audience what it is that he hides in his hand:

> And th' other black and grave, wherewith each one
> Is checker'd all along,
>   *Humilitie:*
> The gentle rising, which on either hand
> Leads to the Quire above,
>   Is *Confidence:*
> But the sweet cement, which in one sure band
> Ties the whole frame, is *Love*
>   And *Charitie*.

This first part of the poem, as Summers has observed,[54] is mechanically emblematic in a way uncharacteristic of Herbert: the relationship between each visual hieroglyph and the moral application wrung from it is not at all obvious, and even when it is revealed, one does not experience the after-the-fact recognition of inevitability so often associated with this poet. This is not to say that any of the

54. *George Herbert,* pp. 124–125. For a different view see Rosemary Freeman, *English Emblem Books* (New York, 1966), p. 163.

equivalences is inapposite, but that someone who has read the first two lines of one of these stanzas would not be able to predict the specifics of the third. This is true even of the third stanza where the revelatory gesture occurs earlier than expected, in line 2, but is then complicated by a further revelation in line 3. As a result, the effect of the stanzas is not cumulative, but additive. The virtues in the interpreter's list—Patience, Humilitie, Confidence, Love, Charitie—remain discreet and isolated because the context within which they are implicated—the context of the floor itself—is significant only in the physical sense suggested by the word "frame" (line 11). Summers remarks that for much of the poem "we are not told to what the floor is being compared" (p. 125), but in these early lines this is a problem we do not even feel, because it does not occur to us that the floor is being compared to anything: it is simply a bounded space, holding in, but in no way shaping, the act of "reading" for which it provides a serial—and potentially endless—form. All this changes with the first word of line 13:

> Hither sometimes Sinne steals, and stains
> The marbles neat and curious veins:
> But all is cleansed when the marble weeps.
> Sometimes Death, puffing at the doore,
> Blows all the dust about the floore:
> But while he thinks to spoil the room, he sweeps.

With "hither," what had been inert and abstract becomes alive. No longer is the church floor simply a backdrop or frame within which significances are adduced; it now becomes the object of an action ("Hither Sinne steals") and in response to that action it weeps. It is here, then, that we first become aware that the floor is being compared to something, and aware too that we do not know what that something is. At once the nature of the reading experience changes: rather than simply receiving meanings we are actively in search of them; but our task is complicated when the object of interpretation refuses to sit still. For fifteen lines our attention has been focused on a simple flat surface, but unexpectedly that surface becomes animate and acquires additional dimensions, first height ("puffing at the doore"), and then depth ("while he thinks to spoil the room"). At the same time that we are asking "what does this mean?" the configurations of "this" are continually changing. The assertive firmness with which the allegory is continued suggests that the answer to the question is obvious (even the rhymes contribute to this suggestion: where before they scarcely registered, they are now strong and pointed), but the clue that would direct us to it is (characteristically) withheld until the final couplet:

> Blest be the *Architect*, whose art
> Could build so strong in a weak heart.

For a moment it seems that one question (to what are the church and its floor being compared?) will simply be replaced by another (who is the architect?), but all questions (even some we had not been asking) are answered by the revelation of the last word. On the most basic level, we discover, as Summers observes, "that the principal referent of the hieroglyph is not the institution of the Church but the human heart" (p. 125). We discover more: we discover that in our search for the significances of the poem's emblems we have been looking everywhere but in the right place; for "heart" not only identifies the first term in a continuing allegory, it at once asks us to *interiorize* that allegory and in so doing to realize the error of our previous interpretive ways. So long as the discerning of a spiritual meaning is considered a problem *external* to an interpreter, that meaning will elude him, just as it eludes the reader of this poem when he seeks it in the physical structure projected by the title. This mis-seeking has, of course, been encouraged by the verse itself; it is part of the strategy by which the reader is brought from what he knows—that the Church rests on a foundation of theological virtues—to what he knows not—that the Church so raised is to be located not in space, but in himself. The conclusion of the poem finds the reader in a position 180 degrees removed from the position he occupied at its beginning, no longer the receiver, but the *repository* of significances; and he is their repository precisely because he has been allowed, for a time, to locate them elsewhere.

"The Church-floore" thus takes its place beside "Love-joy" and "Jesu" as a poem that invites its readers to interpretive activities that are subsequently challenged. They are also (as in "Love-joy" and "Jesu") redeemed; for while it is true that the heart replaces the Church as the hieroglyph's referent, the Church is not thereby dismissed, but resituated; the structures that are distinguished in the moment of the poem's revelation are in the very next moment merged as the collapsing of Church into heart directs the reader to a network of familiar scriptures. The commentary is by Summers:

"The Church-floore" has pictured primarily the marvellous art of God in decreeing the perseverancĕ of Saints rather than His art in the construction of the Church. Yet these two arts are related; once raised, the image of the "Church-floore" as the foundation of Christ's Church is relevant. The final couplet is a dramatic reminder . . . "that the most high dwelleth not in temples made with hands" (Acts vii. 48), "that yee are the Temple of God, and that the Spirit of God dwelleth in you" (1 Cor. iii. 16). But in relation to the subject of the meditation, the title of the poem, the couplet is also a reminder that the structure which God hath built within the heart is truly the "floore" of both the Church Militant and the Church Triumphant; that the conviction within the "weak heart" that "Thou art the Christ, the sonne of the living God" is the "rocke" upon which Christ built his Church. The artful "*Architect*" has built within the individual heart, equally indestructibly, the salvation of the individual and the foundation of His Church. The structure, moreover, is one. Such a complex unfolding of meanings is far removed from the practice of the emblematists, but it is characteristic of Herbert. (p. 126)

My only quarrel with this is that it stops unfolding too soon; for the heart that is the Church's true home is not simply an abstraction to which the poem refers; it is an edifice the poem *raises*, when it brings the reader from one level of illumination to another. "The Church-floore" *performs* the action it describes, building in the weak (misinterpreting) heart of the reader a strong structure of understanding, which, when it is complete, is worthy to be the dwelling place of the architect. That architect is, of course, Jesus Christ, and the revelation of his identity at the poem's conclusion raises a question we can only defer: if Christ is the architect of all such buildings, then is he not the framer of this poem, and responsible for its effects, and does this not place Herbert, as poet-catechist, in the position apparently occupied by his reader-pupil? Simply to ask these questions is to come almost to the end of my story before it has even begun, but the answers must await a fuller delineation of the context in which they will be most meaningful.

We are, of course, constructing this context even now, by examining single poems and finding that, despite obvious differences, they share a great deal, and that what they share can be fairly called catechistical. First of all they share a structure, not of formal or of narrative patterns, but of strategy, a strategy designed to bring the reader, by means of "questions well ordered," to "discover what he is." Moreover in each poem, the content of that discovery is the same because the answer to the questions posed is always the same—Jesus Christ. Indeed, as a model for these poems one need look no further than this example of the parson catechizing:

> . . . the Parson once demanded after other questions about mans misery; since man is so miserable, what is to be done? And the answerer could not tell; He asked him again, what he would do, if he were in a ditch? This familiar illustration made the answer so plaine, that he was even ashamed of his ignorance; for he could not but say, he would hast out of it as fast as he could. Then he proceeded to ask, whether he could get out of the ditch alone, or whether he needed a helper, and who was that helper. (p. 257)

Herbert offers this as an illustration of how the parson makes what his pupil knows "to serve him in that which he knows not." There are two stages in the procedure: first the pupil is made to feel that he has a personal stake in the answering of the question (in this case by being made to feel ashamed of his ignorance), and then he is made to work for that answer, in effect bootstrapping himself up to an insight the parson refuses simply to hand over. It is altogether typical of Herbert that even here, in this instructional manual, his reader is put in the position the prose is describing; for the answer that concludes the sequence is not given (the next sentence begins "This is the skill''), although with only the slightest of efforts (an effort that must however, be expended) every reader will give it, indeed he can not help but give it; this is the art of asking questions. That answer is, of course, "Jesus Christ." He is the helper, just as he is the architect in "The Church-floore," and the meaning both of JC and joy and charity in "Love-joy," and as he is the frame, its content, and the agent of easing in "Jesu." The poems and the catechism teach the same lesson and it is a lesson of personal insufficiency, which, paradoxically, is brought home just when it seems that the reader can claim a success. After false starts and directions too hastily taken, the pupil and/or reader finds the right answer (Jesus Christ), only to find, too, that it is an answer which claims responsibility for its own discovery, and for everything else. The sequence is exactly that reported (and lamented) in the second stanza of "The Crosse":

> And then when after much delay,
> Much wrastling, many a combate, this deare end,
> So much desir'd, is giv'n, to take away
>   My power to serve thee; to unbend
> All my abilities. . . . (lines 7–11)[55]

It is this unbending of abilities that marks Herbert off from the Socrates he describes in *A Priest To the Temple*, the philosopher "who held that the seeds of all truths lay in every body, and accordingly . . . he found Philosophy in silly Trades-men." The reference is to the *Meno*, in which Socrates draws from an ignorant slave boy the laws of geometry; he then proceeds to generalize from his success:

55. See the discussion in S. Fish, *Self-Consuming Artifacts* (Berkeley and Los Angeles, 1972), pp. 183–189.

Socrates: What do you think, Meno? Has he answered with any opinions that were not his own?
Meno: No, they were all his.
Socrates: Yet he did not know, as we agreed a few moments ago.
Meno: True.
Socrates: But these opinions were somewhere in him, were they not?
Meno: Yes.
Socrates: So a man who does not know has in himself true opinions on a subject without having knowledge.
Meno: It would appear so.
Socrates: At present these opinions, being newly aroused, have a dreamlike quality. But if the same questions were put to him on many occasions and in different ways, you can see that in the end he will have a knowledge on the subject as accurate as anybody's.
Meno: Probably.
Socrates: This knowledge will not come from teaching but from questioning. He will recover it for himself. (85 b–d)[56]

It is easy to see why Herbert would be drawn to this passage. The distinction between teaching and questioning parallels the distinction between a catechism that proceeds by rote or examination and one that insists on the involvement of the catechized in his edification; and, for both the philosopher and the poet, success is marked not by the acquiring of new knowledge (that is, of information), but by the more conscious apprehension of knowledge that was always, in some sense, available. It is with respect to the nature of that knowledge, however, that the two diverge: the questioning of the slave boy brings to analytical consciousness something he already knew but only in an inchoate (or "dreamlike") form. The

56. *Meno,* trans. W. K. C. Guthrie, in *Plato: The Collected Dialogues,* ed. Edith Hamilton and Huntington Cairns (Princeton, 1963), p. 370.

movement, then, is from the inside to the outside, from intuition to its explicit formulation. The direction in catechizing is exactly the reverse: the formulation is known (it is written in Scripture) and what the pupil must be led to do is interiorize its significance, discover what it means *for him*; and what he discovers, as we have seen, is that the meaning is self-diminishing. Here, then, is the reason why Socrates' position "will not hold in Christianity" (p. 256); it proclaims the self-sufficiency of the individual ("these opinions were somewhere in him"), whereas the lesson of Herbert's sample catechism (and of his poetry) is that knowledge and salvation come from another. One kind of dialectic draws true opinion from the interlocutor's mind, while the other exposes the insufficiency of that mind to its task and so argues for the necessity of revelation. This is what Herbert means when he declares that Christianity, unlike philosophy, "contains things above nature"; for what is above nature cannot be apprehended by merely natural capacities (including, one must admit, the capacities of the catechist) which must first be disqualified and then transformed. In short, the knowledge to which catechizing brings the pupil is a knowledge of what he does not and cannot, unaided, know; the discovery that awaits him after a succession of "well ordered" questions (and who, one might ask, is responsible for *them?*) is that he is someone who does not have the answers; and if this is a discovery of what he is, then what he is is nothing.[57]

And yet at the same time he is everything, for "know ye not that ye are the temple of God, and that the Spirit of God dwelleth in you?"; the unbending of our abilities,

57. See *Self-Consuming Artifacts,* pp. 174–176.

the taking from us of our ways, is more than compen-
sated for by what we receive in the acknowledgment of
total dependence. ("All things are more ours by their
being His.") The weakness—of will, intellect, faith—
that is exposed by the catechism (and by Herbert's
poetry) is only the other side of the strength we gain,
when, in the full realization that we "can do nought" we
imp our wing on His.[58] The catechistical experience,
then, unfolds in a sequence of three stages: (1) an initial
success, when the pupil finally tumbles (or is driven) to
the right answer, followed by (2) the realization that the
right answer is one that takes away the *personal* satisfaction of having arrived at it (it unbends our abilities), followed by (3) the greater satisfaction awaiting those who
have given everything over to Christ and thus become
members of his perfect body. In the course of the sequence, strength and weakness change places twice,
with the result that finally both are asserted simultaneously. This is precisely the paradox with which "The
Churche-floore" concludes—"build so strong in a weak
heart"—and it is one of the patterns that links Herbert's
poems with each other and marks them as catechistical.
In "Jesu" the frame in the speaker's heart is at once firmly
constructed ("deeply carved") and fragile, and the heart
itself is both broken and whole. The would-be interpreter
in "Love-joy" is off the mark and directly on target at the
same time and with the same response. The building
raised in "The Church-floore" is full of flaws, yet firm
and stable, as is the heart of which it is a hieroglyph. In
"The Windows" man is simultaneously "a brittle crazie
glasse" and "this glorious and transcendent place." And

58. "The Reprisall," line 14; "Easter-wings," line 19.

not only do the poems assert this paradox, they are themselves instances of it: at once disordered and regular,
unfinished and whole.[59]

The paradox, of course, is no paradox at all, since in
each case the weakness, the instability, the incomplete-
ness is predicated of the creature (or his creations), while
the strength, the firmness, the integrity (in the sense of
"having no part or element wanting") is predicated of
God. The heart is strong because its architect supplies its
"natural" deficiencies; the poem is finished when its true
author takes up a faltering pen; "the brittle crazie glasse"
becomes a window through which the light shines on
others, but only "through thy grace" ("The Windows,"
line 5): the spirit of God may dwell in man, but only because that same God has made of man a living temple.[60]

With these observations, we have returned to the question with which this essay began: how is it that the same
body of poetry can be characterized, with equal persua-
siveness, as both restless and secure, precarious and stable, full of surprises and yet perfectly ordered? Two
answers to this question have now been given. The first
involved a transference to the poetry of the distinction
(made in *A Priest To the Temple*) between the perspective
of the catechist, who has "an aim and mark of the whole
discourse . . . in his mind before any question be propounded," and the perspective of the catechized who is
"driven" to that mark by a route whose ways will seem
indirect and fortuitous (loose and wild). In the context of
this formula, the conflicting characterizations of Herbert's poetry can be accommodated: the poetry is tentative

59. See, among others, "Deniall," "A True Hymne," "The Altar,"
"The Forerunners."
60. See "Sion" and "Man."

and provisional because the reader's experience of it is marked by false starts and premature conclusions, but it is also controlled and assured because the artificer of that experience knows exactly what he is doing. What he is doing is moving the reader toward a moment of self-discovery and it is from the nature of that discovery that we have derived a second answer to our question: because the aim of the discourse is always the realization of one's dependence on Jesus Christ, the reader's success will be inseparable from an acknowledgement of personal inadequacy, and that, in turn, will be preliminary to the larger success awaiting him in a union (effected by grace) with God. ("In thee I will overcome.")[61] In this union, the perfection of one party will be extended to supply the defects of the other who therefore will at the same time be everything and nothing, that is, at once secure and precariously unstable. The collective intuition of Herbert criticism is thus affirmed by arguments that are both formal and substantive. It should be noted, however, that at a crucial point these arguments pull against one another: the catechistical formula allows us to reconcile the contradictory judgments on the poetry by dividing them between the poet and his reader, but as a result the poet is placed in a position which, in terms of the lesson he teaches, is reserved solely for God. It would seem that placing *The Temple* in a catechistical context solves problems at one level only to reintroduce them at another.

I do not mean to suggest that my case is proven, even on the most basic level of demonstrating influence. All I have been able to show is that, first, Herbert's view of

61. "The Reprisall," line 15.

catechizing is unlike that of his contemporaries because it gives the pupil a large and necessary role in his own edification and that, second, by moving back and forth between Herbert's remarks on catechizing and his poetry one is able to make sense of what would otherwise remain a critical puzzle. It is one thing, however, to argue that such a move is helpful, and quite another to demonstrate that it is warranted. What, in short, is my evidence?

One kind of evidence is available in the poems themselves, especially in those places where Herbert speaks of his hopes for them. Here we may take as a central text the final stanza of "Obedience":

> How happie were my part,
> If some kinde man would thrust his heart
> Into these lines; till in heav'ns Court of Rolls
> They were by winged souls
> Entred for both, farre above their desert! (lines 41–45)

I would cite lines like these to support the inferential structure of my argument: that is, since Herbert thought seriously enough about catechizing to depart from the views of his contemporaries (although, as I shall show, he has sources in the early liturgy and in the Fathers), and since what distinguishes his view is an intention to move the auditor rather than simply to examine him, and since this is precisely the intention he announces in the poetry, is it not then reasonable to apply what is said of one activity to the other? A less conjectural inference can be drawn from the opening stanza of "The Church-porch":

> Thou, whose sweet youth and early hopes inhance
> Thy rate and price, and mark thee for a treasure;
> Hearken unto a Verser, who may chance
> Ryme thee to good, and make a bait of pleasure.

> A verse may find him, who a sermon flies,
> And turn delight into a sacrifice.

The terms in which poetry is praised here are the terms in which catechizing is praised in *A Priest To the Temple:* "At Sermons . . . men may sleep or wander; but when one is asked a question, he must discover what he is" (p. 257). It is not simply that in both texts a comparison is made at the expense of sermons, but that the virtues of poetry and catechizing are the same: they do not allow the reader-auditor to be passive; he is "found," he is "discovered," he is drawn in, and once in, he is asked to make a sacrifice, that is, to perform both an act of holiness (a communion) and an act of submission.

These are also the virtues that were attributed to the poetry in Herbert's own century when testimony credited the poet with "many pious converts."[62] Crashaw is not only drawn in, but would extend the benefits by sending "Mr. Herbert's book" to another. She, in turn, is warned that one cannot read these poems passively: "Know you faire, on what you looke; / Divinest love lyes in this book: / Expecting fire from your eyes, / To kindle this his sacrifice."[63] Christopher Harvey is moved to build a synagogue in imitation of *The Temple*

62. *The Works of Henry Vaughan,* ed. L. C. Martin (Oxford, 1957), p. 391. Even if Walton is writing hagiography, his report of Herbert's directions to Ferrar at the very least reflects an accepted view of the poet's intention: "Desire him [Ferrar] to read it, and then if he can think it may turn to the advantage of any dejected poor Soul, let it be made publick; if not, let him burn it" (*The Life of Mr. George Herbert,* London, 1970, p. 74).

63. "On Mr. G. Herberts booke intituled the Temple of Sacred Poems, sent to a Gentlewoman," in *Crashaw's Poetical Works,* ed. L. C. Martin (Oxford, 1927), p. 130.

as a raiser of souls: "These holy Hymns had an Ethereal birth; / For they can raise sad souls above the earth, / And fix them there, / Free from the world's anxieties and fear. / *Herbert* and you have pow'r / To do this: Ev'ry hour I read you, kills a sin / Or lets a virtue in."[64] An even more eloquent witness is Henry Vaughan who speaks for others as well as for himself when he attests to the effects of Herbert's "holy ever-living lines":

> Dear friend! whose holy, ever-living lines
> Have done much good
> To many, and have checkt my blood,
> My fierce, wild blood that still heaves, and inclines,
> But is still tam'd
> By those bright fires which thee inflam'd;
> Here I joyn hands, and thrust my stubborn heart
> Into thy *Deed*.
>
> ("The Match," lines 1–8)

Vaughan is only one of many who declare themselves to be the realization of the hopes Herbert expresses in "Obedience." In a commendatory poem written for the tenth edition of *The Temple* (1674), an anonymous admirer asks, "What Father of a Church; can you rehearse, / That gain'd more Souls to God, 'twixt Prose and Verse?"[65] Here, no distinction is made between the poetry and the prose because the important thing about Herbert's words, in either form, is what they do, and what they do, according to William Dillingham, is "pour and . . . breathe true piety into the mind of the

---

64. "To my Reverend Friend The Author of 'The Synagogue,'" in R. H. Ray, *George Herbert in the Seventeenth Century: Allusions to Him Collected and Annotated*, Diss. University of Texas at Austin (1967). Hereafter cited as Ray, followed by the appropriate page number.
    65. Ray, p. 192.

reader."[66] That mind, in turn, is called to strenuous activity, for as J. L. observes in 1647, Herbert's "every strain / Twists holy breasts."[67] The breast that is not holy is made so, since like a "wise physician," Joshua Poole tells us, Herbert is able to "Cozen unwilling Patients into health."[68] Indeed so powerful is the medicine of his art, that at the end of the century Nahum Tate is claiming for it the power "of reclaiming even profligate Persons."[69]

This enumeration of testimonies could be extended indefinitely, but the point, I trust, has been made: Herbert's poetry was not simply read, it was used, "frequently quoted," as one unknown divine remarks, "in Sermons and other Discourses,"[70] turned into hymns (by that same divine), and made the basis for the instruction of the young. This last is most significant, since instruction for the young is what catechisms, by definition, are. When Henry Delaune wanted to leave a legacy of precepts ("Theological, Moral, Political, Oecenomical") to his sons, he cited "Divine Herbert" as a model, reminding his reader that "'*A Verse may finde Him, Who, a Sermon, flies.*'"[71] Schoolmasters regularly recommend Mr. Herbert's poems, "most worthy," says Charles Hoole, "to be mentioned in the first place."[72] In 1695, a writer to the *Athenian Mercury* asks *"What Books of Poetry wou'd you Advise one that's Young?"* and is told to read, among other things in a short list, David's Psalms and Herbert's poems.[73] Herbert and the psalmist are often linked in the century (in 1697 Daniel Baker calls the poet "Our *David*, our sweet psalmist . . . who a Temple built"),[74] a pairing

66. Ray, p. 218.
67. Ray, p. 64.
68. Ray, p. 136.
69. Ray, p. 266.
70. Ray, p. 269.
71. Ray, p. 89.
72. Ray, p. 148.
73. Ray, p. 261.
74. Ray, pp. 313–314.

that is particularly significant since David was considered the very type of the catechist. [75] What has been called the earliest Anglican anthology of poetry for children contains a number of Herbert's lyrics, and the anthology in turn is appended to a volume that bears this title: *The key of knowledge, opening the principles of religion; and the path of life, directing the practice of true pietie: design'd for the conduct of children and servants, in the right way to heaven and happiness.* [76] If the thesis of this study has any merit, it is a nice symmetry to find Herbert's catechistical poems turning up in a catechism.

It would be premature, however, to claim that symmetry, for the evidence I have marshaled is still circumstantial. In an age whose concerns are so pervasively religious, it would be surprising only if we did *not* find points of contact between a body of devotional poetry and the catechism; that is, the relationship may well be an over-determined one and not an instance of cause and effect. The argument from Herbert's reputation is even less conclusive, since at the very most it proves something about what people made of Herbert's poetry rather than something about what Herbert's poetry is made of. What is required, of course, is evidence that in putting together *The Temple* Herbert had catechistical models in mind, and it is evidence of this kind that I hope to provide

75. See Barnabas Oley in Ray, p. 107: "In summ, . . . Master *Herbert* [is] like David"; Donne, *Sermons,* vol. IX, 251: "So great a Master as *David,* proceeded by way of Catechisme"; Andrewes, *A patterne* (1675), p. 1: "King David, who being at one time (among others) determined to catechize Children, calls them to him, saying, Come ye Children and hearken unto me . . . a plain preface before catechizing." See also Heather Asals, "The Voice of George Herbert's 'The Church,'" *ELH,* 36 (1969), 511–517.

76. Ray, p. 244.

in the following pages. The case will be presented at length and in great detail, but essentially it will involve the unpacking of a single assertion from *A Priest To the Temple:* the end of catechizing, we are told, is to infuse a competent knowledge of salvation in every one of the parson's flock so that he can then proceed to "build up this knowledge to a spirituall Temple."

Two: Work To Be Done/Work Already Done: The Rhetoric Of Templehood

1. THE FOUNDATIONS

My THESIS can be stated simply: the temple of Herbert's title is the "spirituall Temple" that is built up by catechisms to be the dwelling place of God. Others have identified that place with something the poems image or present: I will argue that it is something they would create, not on the page or in space, but in the heart of the reader. This argument has already been partly made with reference to the strategy of particular poems, and I would now like to extend it to the whole. My model is "The Church-floore," a poem that is paradigmatic in several respects:

1. It presents an architectural metaphor that is subsequently internalized.
2. The metaphor has reference finally to the building of

a structure in the heart, or to the building of the heart into a certain kind of structure.

3. Just such a structure is built up in the heart of the reader who enters the poem in search of significances (that is what a reader *does*) and finds in the end that he himself is their repository.

"Know ye not that ye are the temple of God, and that the Spirit of God dwelleth in you?" asks the apostle. It is to that knowledge and therefore to that condition—of being a temple—that this sequence of poems is intended to bring us.

Of course, one may so characterize *The Temple* without invoking the label "catechistical." What evidence is there to link the rearing of this particular temple (either the poem or the structure it raises) to the forms and concerns of the catechism? The remainder of this essay will be given over to answering that question, and we can begin by documenting the existence of a tradition in which there is a commonplace association between catechizing and temple building. This association has a long and complex history, but in order to establish it we need look no further than the first few pages of any Reformation catechism. Here, for example, is the prayer that introduces John Mayer's catechism (the abridged version) in 1623:

Thou which art the Master-builder of thine owne house, settle me as one of thy living stones upon the right foundation, Jesus Christ; in whom I may daily grow up, till that all the building coupled together, groweth to an holy Temple in the Lord.[1]

This prayer is a conflation of several biblical texts, all of

1. *Mayers catechisme abridged,* second edition (1623).

which are regularly cited by catechists as providing authority and direction for their labors. These texts are joined by a concern with Christian education and by the architectural metaphor they use to describe the course of that education:

(19) Now, therefore, ye are no more strangers and foreigners, but fellow citizens with the saints, and of the household of God; (20) And are built upon the foundation of the apostles and prophets, Jesus Christ himself being the chief corner stone; (21) In whom all the building fitly framed together groweth unto an holy temple in the Lord; (22) In whom ye also are builded together for an habitation of God through the Spirit. (Ephesians 2:19–22)

(11) And he gave some, apostles; and some, prophets; and some, evangelists; and some, pastors and teachers; (12) For the perfecting of the saints, for the work of the ministry, for the edifying of the body of Christ: (13) Till we all come in the unity of the faith, and of the knowledge of the Son of God, unto a perfect man, unto the measure of the stature of the fulness of Christ: (14) That we henceforth be no more children, tossed to and fro, and carried about with every wind of doctrine. . . . (15) But speaking the truth in love, may grow up into him in all things, which is the head, even Christ. (Ephesians 4:11–15)

(2) As newborn babes, desire the sincere milk of the word, that ye may grow thereby; (3) If so be ye have tasted that the Lord is gracious. (4) To whom coming, as unto a living stone, disallowed indeed of men but chosen of God and precious, (5) Ye also, as lively stones, are built up a spiritual house, an holy priesthood, to offer up spiritual sacrifices, acceptable to God by Jesus Christ. (6) Wherefore also it is contained in the scripture, Behold, I lay in Sion a chief cornerstone, elect, precious; and he that believeth on him shall not be confounded. (I Peter 2:2–6)

(9) For we are labourers together with God: ye are God's husbandry, ye are God's building. (10) According to the grace of God which is given unto me, as a wise masterbuilder, I have laid the foundations, and another buildeth thereon. But let

every man take heed how he buildeth thereupon. (11) For other foundation can no man lay than that is laid, which is Jesus Christ. . . . (16) Know ye not that ye are the temple of God, and that the Spirit of God dwelleth in you? (17) If any man defile the temple of God, him shall God destroy; for the temple of God is holy, which temple ye are. (I Corinthians 3:9–11, 16–17)

These passages contain not one but three metaphors. Those who are addressed by Paul and Peter are characterized variously as plants that are watered ("I have planted, Apollos watered; but God gave the increase"), as bodies that are nourished ("desire the sincere milk of the word, that ye may grow thereby"), and as buildings that are raised. Each of these metaphors figures importantly in catechistical rhetoric, but the third is by far the most prominent. "It is a common title," E. B. tells us, that "the principles of religion . . . are called grounds, which is a very fit appelation [since] all such who are not skilled in these principles are as a building which stands upon no firme ground."[2] Catechizing, says Robert Allen, is often "compared . . . to the laying of the foundation of a building." "Of this building," he continues, "Christ onely is the foundation: yea the whole building riseth to perfection in him 1.Cor.3.11. and Ephes.4.11.12.13."[3] "Who doubteth," asks Samuel Crooke, "but that even by this kind of teaching . . . the Saints [are] gathered and built up together into the body of Christ?"[4] Lancelot Andrewes rehearses the same commonplace—"The course of Religion we are to treat of is likened to a building"— and then proceeds to elaborate it: "hee which is to teach is

2. *A Catechisme or Briefe Instruction in the Principles and Grounds of the true Christian Religion. With a short Treatise premised concerning the profit and necessity of Catechizing* (1617), sigs. A5^v–A6^r.

3. *A treasurie of catechisme, or christian instruction* (1600), p. 2.

4. *The guide unto true blessednesse*, sig. B5^r.

likened to a builder: the principles of Religion are called a foundation; that must be digged deepe, till wee come to the Rocke, that our building may not be shallow upon the earth without foundation."[5]

Obviously, then, the metaphor is firmly established, but at the same time it is also unstable. First of all, it is not clear whether the building in question is the catechism (as it seems to be for Andrewes) or the interior structure whose raising it effects. An even more fundamental ambiguity resides in the word "building" itself, which can either be a noun, and therefore indicative of a state, or a participle, and therefore indicative of a process. In E. B.'s formulation, the comparison is between two buildings that are already standing; the metaphor, then, is spatial. For Allen, on the other hand, the dimension of the comparison is temporal: catechizing is the first of many stages in the construction (that is, building) of a building. When Andrewes speaks of likening the catechizing to a building, the word could be either noun (spatial) or participle (temporal), and the ambiguity is maintained throughout his text ("that our building may not be shallow"). T. W[alkington], on the other hand, shows his awareness of the ambiguity by the care he takes to avoid it. He is commenting on Hebrews 6:1 ("leaving the principles of the doctrine of Christ, let us go on unto perfection, not laying again the foundation") and responding to the question: *"Wherefore doth [the apostle] call the doctrine of the Catechisme a Foundation?"* The answer comes in two stages: this, he says, is "a figurative speech taken from earthly affaires, as from buildings." Here "buildings" is obviously nominal and refers to two standing structures; but in the explication of the figure, the word becomes a

5. *A patterne of catechisticall doctrine*, pp. 13–14.

verbal and it is understood that the structure has only begun to be raised: "Even so in the spirituall building up of mens consciences to God, the doctrine of Catechisme is first to be laid as a foundation and afterward the misterie of Christ is more highly and deeply to bee handled."[6] T. W. delimits the meaning of "building" because in his view the catechism is only a preliminary and elementary kind of instruction ("it containes the . . . A B C of Christianitie"), but other catechists are less modest, and they find the equivocation at the heart of the metaphor useful and attractive. Since the same word serves to designate both a process and its achieved goal, the catechist is able to make claims that are at once limited and very large. That is, he can characterize his activity as a mere beginning, as the first step in a building (participle), and yet suggest (without asserting) that it is a beginning that contains its end, a building (noun).

A similar strategy can be pursued if one turns to the other great metaphor of catechistical rhetoric in which the first principles are compared not to a foundation but to milk. Here the catechist is able to maneuver in the space between two of the other texts that appear often on his title pages:

For when for the time ye ought to be teachers, ye have need that one teach you again which be the first principles of the oracles of God; and are become such as have need of milk, and not of strong meat. (Hebrews 5:12)

As newborn babes, desire the sincere milk of the word, that ye may grow thereby. (I Peter 2:2)

6. *An exposition of the two first verses of the sixt chapter to the Hebrewes in forme of a Dialogue. Wherin You Have A commendation of Catechising, Also a declaration of the sixe fundamentall Principles, wherin the Christians of the Primitive Apostolicall Church were Catechised* (1609), pp. 1–2.

As Calvin points out, in Hebrews (and also in I Corinthians 3:1) "*Milk* is called the simpler mode of teaching, and one suitable to children where there is no progress made beyond the first rudiments," but in I Peter:

> milk . . . is not elementary doctrine . . . but a mode of living which has the savor of a new birth, when we surrender ourselves to be brought up by God. In the same manner *infancy* is not set in opposition to manhood, or to the full grown man in Christ (as Paul calls him in Eph. 4.13), but to the old age of the flesh and of the old life. Moreover, as the infancy of the new life is perpetual, so Peter recommends milk as a perpetual nourishment for he wishes those nourished by it to grow.[7]

In one interpretation of the metaphor, catechisms are intended only for children; in the other, they provide nourishment the need for which is never outgrown. Just as the ambiguity in building allows the catechist to claim for his labors the status both of a beginning and a goal, so the two readings of "milk" allow him to claim a constituency larger than the one (apparently) named in his title: *Milk for Babes*. Quotations from I Peter and Hebrews 5 adorn the title pages of catechisms as if there were no distinction to be made between them; but there is a distinction (Calvin makes it) or, rather, an ambiguity, and if the catechists do not acknowledge it openly, they acknowledge (and make use of) it implicitly by including in the category "catechism" not only brief documents or "summes" no longer than the questions and answers in the Book of Common Prayer, but full-fledged tracts of divinity, in some cases more than 700 pages long. Calvin considered his *Institutes* a catechistical work which grew

7. *The Epistle of Paul The Apostle to the Hebrews and The First and Second Epistles of St. Peter. Calvin's New Testament Commentaries,* trans. William B. Johnson (Eerdmans), p. 257.

with each successive edition, and it is his example among others that allows Daniel Featly to insist that this way of teaching serves not only to instruct the young and ignorant, but to "confirme the learned in the principles of Religion."[8]

One can see, then, that the instability of the "milk" and "building" metaphors is, in some ways, their chief recommendation; and yet in another way that same instability threatens the project these metaphors support by calling into question its independence. This threat is implicit in Anthony Burgesse's commentary on I Corinthians 3:9, "ye are God's building." The word "building," he says, does "seem to comprehend bothe the matter, and Gods action about it; . . . we are the *house* of God, and . . . the *building* also is of God; . . . we are of God both *in fieri* and *facto esse.*"[9] That is, we are at once rising into God and already made of, and by, Him. The equivocation between "building" as a participle and "building" as a noun is also an equivocation between work that is yet to be done and work that stands already accomplished. It thus poses a danger to the "building" metaphor at the very point where the catechists find it most attractive; that is, at the point where it legitimizes their efforts by suggesting that they are necessary. From the beginning catechists use the

8. *The summe of saving knowledge* (1626), p. 2. On this point, see Jeremias Bastingius, *An exposition or commentarie upon the catechisme of Christian religion* (1595), sig. A4^{v}; William Basset, *A discourse on my lord-archbiship's of Canterbury's . . . Letters* (1684), pp. 7–8; Richard Bernard, *The common catechisme* (1630), sig. A4^{v}; John Boughton, *God and man* (1623), p. 3; Samuel Crooke, *The guide*, sigs. B5^{v}, C2^{v}; Henry Holland, *The historie of Adam or the foure-fold State of Man* (1606), pp. 2–3. Featly (*The summe*, sig. A3^{r}) declares that "true Divinity is nothing but *Catechismus explicatus, Catechising at large.*"

9. *The Scripture directory, For Church-Officers and People* (1659), p. 117.

metaphor not only to characterize what they do, but to warn of the danger of not doing it. Cyril of Jerusalem (C. 315–386) can stand for all the catechists who follow him:

> . . . let me compare the catechizing to a building. Unless we methodically bind and joint the whole structure together, we shall have leaks and dry rot, and all our previous exertions will be wasted. No: stone must be laid upon stone in regular sequence, and corner follow corner, jutting edges must be planed away: and so the perfect structure rises.[10]

Lancelot Andrewes, who cites Cyril as his source, complains: "The builders of our age digge not deepe enough; they digge not to the Rocke" (p. 14); J. Syme is worried lest he who builds on an unsure foundation "shall not only lose his cost and travell spent about it, but also endanger his life in it, by the unexpected tumbling of it down about his hed."[11] John Frewen assures his readers that without the foundation provided by catechizing, "whatsoever is builded thereupon cannot possibly stand . . . ready with every blast of winde to be overturned."[12] With Cyril and a host of others, these catechists strongly imply that were they not to perform their duties ("Unless we methodically bind and joint the whole structure together"), the "perfect structure" would fail to rise.

In Ephesians, Corinthians, Peter, and Hebrews, however, the perfect structure has already risen (in several senses), and therefore the labors to which the catechists

10. *The Works of Saint Cyril of Jerusalem*, vol. I, trans. L. P. McCauley, S.J., and A. A. Stephenson (Washington, 1969), p. 79.

11. *The sweet milke of christian doctrine* (1617), sig. A2ʳ.

12. *Certaine choise grounds, and principles of our Christian religion* (1621), pp. 5–6.

urge themselves and their pupils have a problematical status. Catechists are to lay the foundation, but "other foundations can no man lay than that is laid," i.e., than that which is *already* laid. On those same foundations we will grow "unto an holy temple," but "the temple of God is holy, which temple ye [already] are." "Be ye builded together," declares Paul, but does he intend an exhortation, or a statement of (accomplished) fact? Calvin asks that question and finds that the phrase is ambiguous, in two languages:

The Greek ending, like that of the Latin (*coedificamini*) is ambiguous. For both the imperative and indicative mood would fit, and the context will admit either.[13]

The imperative and indicative correspond precisely to the two forms of building, the first indicating a process that may, like any other, go wrong, the second, a state, achieved and secure, and therefore independent of what any group of men may or may not do.

In this passage from Ephesians and in the other passages regularly cited by catechists, two mutually exclusive explanatory paradigms sit side by side. The tension between them is reflected in what we might call the narrative "progress" of these passages. They read superficially almost as sets of directions, telling us how to put something together (in this case the Temple of God) in stages, but the stages, while continuous on the page, and even linked by a syntax, are finally radically discontinuous, because at each of them the relationship between (and even the identity of) agent, materials, and goal,

13. *The Epistles of Paul The Apostle to the Galatians, Ephesians, Philippians and Colossians. Calvin's New Testament Commentaries*, trans. T. H. L. Parker (Eerdmans), p. 156.

64 The Living Temple

changes. In verses 19 and 20 of Ephesians 2, that relationship seems quite clear; the citizens addressed by Paul will be built, by his efforts and the efforts of the other apostles, into a religious community, a "household of God," and Jesus Christ will be the cornerstone of that house. But in verse 21, that cornerstone, rather than being one component of the building (participle and noun), is the context in which that building (participle) goes on; and moreover it is no longer a building (itself ambiguous between process and state), but a growth: "In whom all the building fitly framed together groweth." Without any announcement, a mechanical metaphor has become organic, an intermittent and fitful procedure has been replaced by a teleology. But that teleology is no more stable than the sequence in which it suddenly appeared. As Matthew Poole observes, "groweth" can be read as "either 1. *ariseth;* the Building goeth on till it come to be a Temple. Or 2. it notes the Stones or Materials of the House to be living ones, receiving life from Christ."[14] In other words, the building is either in the process of becoming God's temple, or it is growing precisely because it is already informed by his spirit. "Grow" is also ambiguous in another way: it can either mean "grow up to," in the sense of rising to be a free standing structure, or "grow into" (or unto) in the sense of becoming a part of, by disappearing into, a structure that is already standing. In verse 21 it is first one, when the citizens are promised that they will rise into "an holy temple," and then the other, when the temple is revealed to be not *for,* but "*in* the Lord." That phrase, too, admits of more than one

14. *Annotations Upon the Holy Bible* (1696), sig. Qqq2ʳ. See also John Coolidge, *The Pauline Renaissance in England* (Oxford, 1970), pp. 23–54.

interpretation: "it may be joined with *Holy*," Poole points out, "and then it signifies that they have their Holiness from Christ, or it may be read Holy *to* the Lord, and then it expresses the nature of this Temple, that it is undefiled, consecrated to the Lord, and meet for him." That is, either meet for him or made meet for him by him. It is in the context of these possibilities that we come upon the words "ye also are builded." The ambiguity noted by Calvin, between the imperative urgency attending a project whose success is uncertain and the indicative assertion of that project's already being complete, is only one more variation of an ambiguity that is present everywhere in the passage. It finds still another variation in the words "through the Spirit," and once again, Poole's commentary is evidence of how attentive Reformation readers were to the discontinuities we have been noting: "This may relate either to the words immediately going before, *an Habitation of God*, and then the meaning is, an Habitation or Temple in which God dwells by his Spirit; or to the Verb Builded, and then they import the building of them into a Temple to be the operation of the Spirit." As the sequence ends, the perfect structure has in fact risen, not however into its own form, but into the form of another, into the "perfect man," Jesus Christ, whose perfection antedates the builders' exertions and cannot receive any addition from what they (appear to) build.

It seems clear that this text and the others that share its vocabulary (of temples, stones, members, and foundations) are *radically* ambiguous, indeterminate not at one point, but at every point, whether the question is one of agency—Who is doing what to whom? Or sequence—When did something happen and in relation to what antecedent and subsequent events? Or the nature of the materials—Are they inert or alive? Or the characterization of the phenomenon itself—Is it a building (participle) or a building (noun), contingent or necessary, mechanical or organic, static or dynamic? These questions are all related because they are all generated by the single large ambiguity of which each smaller ambiguity is a variant or transformation: *work to be done/work already done.* Is the raising of the "spirituall Temple" a mechanical task subject to all the errors flesh is heir to, or is it a task accomplished before the beginning of time, which functions only to provide a succession of spaces for its certain unfolding? The phrase "temple of God," standing as it does at the center of these texts, does not resolve the ambiguity, but relocates it in a preposition. Are we "of" God in the sense that we are consecrated to him, opening our doors to him but to no other (this places the responsibility for our status squarely on us), or are we "of" God in the stronger sense of being his work, temples made not only for him to dwell in, but made of him ("other foundation can no man lay"), as opposed, say, to being made of wood or stone or gold (this places the responsibility for our status squarely on him, and therefore makes it independent of temporal accidents). The same question could be asked of the temple's components: are the stones that are to be built up (another ambiguity: is some other substance to be built up into fit stones, or are already fit stones to be built up into a temple?) materials apart from God or are they "of him"? In I Peter they are both, and therefore neither, when the living stone is first Christ and then those who are to come unto him. Can we become living stones (is this an imperative) or are we made living stones (is it an indicative)?

Henry Ainsworth, in his commentary on the passage, simply offers both readings, one after the other. It is our duty, he declares, "that we carry our selves as living stones in his spirituall house which is his Church, he that is Christs must be a new creature . . . for unlesse we come to Christ by faith, we shall depart from him without fruit."[15] Here is all the urgency (all the imperative) that an apologist for catechizing could desire; the possibility of failure is also the possibility of independence (i.e., that we *could* depart from him), but both possibilities are short-circuited when Ainsworth says in the very next sentence (his sequences are also discontinuous): "He is a living stone and he makes us living stones." An ambiguous text is ambiguously interpreted, hermeneutics merely reproducing the conditions that call it into being. Wherever one looks in these texts one finds instability, not of the simple and comforting kind that offers itself as an ontology, but of a kind that operates to prevent interpretive rest. One would think that interpretive rest would be provided by Jesus Christ; but it is precisely his appearance in these texts that interrupts and reverses their narrative progress by making it impossible to distinguish cause from effect, agent from material, beginning from end. Rather than mediating between contradictions or resolving paradoxes, Christ literally embodies them ("In whom all the building fitly framed together groweth unto an holy temple in the Lord"), and this is only surprising if we forget that it is his own ambiguous nature—God or man, word or flesh, temporal or eternal—which generates them.

It is not surprising that catechistical rhetoric, which is

15. *Certain notes of Mr. Henry Ainsworth, his last sermon* (1630), sig. A8^v.

so dependent on these texts, should have at its heart the ambiguity that informs them. One sees it as early as Cyril, who (as Andrewes notes) concludes his preface by exhorting the catechumens to make their house of the right materials, but then reminding them that, after all, while he may speak and they may act, it is God who accomplishes the work (*"Meum est dicere, tuum vero, agere, Dei autem perficere"*).[16] Cyril is thus in the same position occupied by Paul and Peter in the texts he cites; he gives out instructions ("these, then are the instructions, these the battle orders, that I . . . give to you")[17] for a task that may well have been already accomplished. Those whom he instructs inherit his precarious situation, urged, as they are, to labors (of self-edification) only another can perform, and, indeed, *has performed*. The enterprise, as it is handed down from father to son and from teacher to pupil, can never outrun the contradiction that threatens it, because that contradiction is built into its very foundations, which are not its own. It is the same contradiction that we shall find at the heart of Herbert's poetry, even as we have already found it reproduced in the criticism: that is, in its equivocation between a structure that is precarious, shifting, and unfinished (work to be done) and a structure that is firm, secure, and complete (work already done).

2. WHEREVER GOD DWELLS, THERE IS HIS TEMPLE

This last observation has brought us once again to the larger issues of this study, but I propose now to back

16. *Catecheses Illuminatorum Hierosulymis XVIII & quinque Mystagogicae*, ed. J. Groedicus (Cologne, 1564), p. 7.

17. *The Works of Saint Cyril*, vol. I, p. 84.

away from them in order to pursue a limited point: in the
period 1540 to 1640 when one thinks of catechizing, one
thinks of temples. The connection is so firmly established
that it is difficult to determine the direction of influence:
catechists regularly allude on their title pages and in their
prefaces to those scriptures concerned with the edifying
of Christians into living temples (Ephesians 2:20 appears
on the title pages of the French, Latin, and English editions of Calvin's catechism), and commentators on those
same scriptures in turn identify the builders of I Corinthians, I Peter, and Hebrews, and the teachers of Ephesians as catechists. T. W. does not even bother to assert
the association; it simply becomes a presupposition of his
second question: *"Wherefore dothe he [Paul] call the doctrine
of the Catechisme a Foundation?"* Niels Hemmingsen is
more expository, but his commentary, in its very brevity
and flatness, tells us that in his own mind he is delivering
a commonplace: "They are (Teachers), whom the Church
in olde time called by the name of Catechisers: whose
office was to set downe a forme and order of doctrine,
and to deliver certaine foundations."[18]

By attaching themselves to the "temple-building"
metaphor the catechists also fall heir to the multiple contexts it invades, that is, to the multiple referents available
for the word "temple." The most important of these are
enumerated in Nicholas Byfield's commentary on I Peter
2:5, "Ye also, as lively stones, are built up a spiritual
house, an holy priesthood."

And thus Christ calleth his owne body a Temple, *John* 2.21 . . .
the heart of man is the Tabernacle of Christ: and so both the
whole Catholique Church is his Tabernacle, Eph. 2.21, or the
publick assembly of the Saints, Psalm 15.1 or else the heart of

18. *The Epistle of the Blessed Apostle* (1580), p. 138.

every particular beeliever: and so the power of Christ did rest upon *Paul* as in a Tabernacle 2 *Cor*. 12.9. So are we said to be the Temple of God. [19]

Byfield's "So are we said" refers to the entire passage of which it is a conclusion. We are the temple of God in all these ways, as individual believers in whose hearts Christ dwells, as communicants in his visible temple, "the whole Catholique Church," as one of the assembly of saints, that is, of the Church Militant, and as members of his perfect body, the temple that has always stood and will continue to stand. There are, then, as Joseph Hall observes, "four temples," and yet "it is but one in matter . . . as the God that dwells in it is one . . . for wherever God dwells, there is his temple."[20] These temples are often opposed to the material temple built by Solomon, for "it is not," says Paul Baynes, "a materiall house which is a temple for God":

He is a spirit, and as *Solomon* confesses in the dedication; and as *Isa*. 66. The *spirit of the humble and contrite men*, fearing before him, they are the *fittest houses for him*: and the materiall Temple was symbolicall, such as had reference to a further thing which it signified, that is 1. the Humanity of Christ, the Temple of the God-head, in the true Immanuel. 2. The multitude of the faithfull here in this place. 3. Every particular believer, I *Cor*. 3. 16.[21]

19. *A commentary; or sermons upon the second chapter of the first epistle of Peter* (1623), pp. 149–150.

20. *The Works of Bishop Hall*, vol. I, ed. J. Pratt (London, 1808), p. 437.

21. *A commentary upon the epistle* (1642), p. 329. See Burgesse, *The Scripture directory*, p. 197: "This [Ye] may be taken both *collectively*, as a *Church*, a Community a society; as the Temple was not one stone, but a multitude of stones artificially built together. And Secondly *Distributively*. [Ye] that is, *every man* is the Temple of the Holy ghost." See also Niels Hemmingsen, *The Epistle of the Blessed Apostle*, p. 100: "Here the reason must be marked, why the whole Church of God is called (One temple:) and why everie severall beleever, is named (The livelie temple

The rhetoric of this passage, and of countless others like it, goes in two directions: on the one hand, the various temples are distinguished and arranged in a hierarchy ("they are the *fittest houses for him*"), but on the other, they are collapsed into one another by the informing spirit that gives each of them life ("for wherever God dwells, there is his temple"). These temples, then, are simultaneously many and one, different and the same, and they are therefore available to any number of organizations, to momentary oppositions, and equally momentary allegiances. Baynes's point is that God prefers some temples to others, and the three preferred temples are presented indifferently. Matthew Poole, on the other hand, wants to be sure that the institutional temple is not emphasized at the expense of the personal, and the structure of his sentence reflects that concern: "Not only the whole Collection of believers is called the Temple of God, but particular Churches, and particular Saints are so called, because of God's dwelling in them by his Spirit."[22] Hall, in his *Contemplations*, moves in the opposite direction, from individual to community, and forward in time, from the temple of the Church Militant, to the temple of the Church Triumphant. Indeed, in a single passage he rings almost all the changes made possible by the fluidity of the metaphor:

---

of God) in like case. The whole Church is therefore called the temple of God, both because it is reared up and built upon one foundation: and also because all the faithful being joined together in the unitie of faith and love, have God dwelling in them. . . . Every severall Christian is therefore called the livelie temple of God, both for that everie of them is builded upon one onelie foundation, which is the Lord Jesus Christ; and also, for that God dwelleth in everie of them."

22. *Annotations*, sig. Qqq2^{v}.

O God, thou vouchsafest to dwell in the believing heart . . . and, for that the most general division of the saints is their place and estate, some struggling and toiling in this earthly warfare, others triumphing in heavenly glory, therefore hath God two more universal temples; one the Church of his saints on earth; the other, the highest Heaven of his saints glorified. In all of these, O God, thou dwellest for ever, and this material house of thine is a clear representation of these three spiritual. . . . And though one of these was a true type of all, yet how are they all exceeded each by other! This of stone, though more rich and costly, yet what is it to the living temple of the Holy Ghost, which is our body? What is the temple of this body of ours, to the temple of Christ's body, which is his Church? And what is the temple of God's Church on earth, to that which triumpheth gloriously in heaven? (p. 437)

In the distinction between the temple of the Church Militant (made up of those still toiling) and the temple of the Church Triumphant (made of those already glorified) we find still another reinscription of the contradiction (work to be done/work already done) that gives these texts their energy. Like the other distinctions in this extraordinary sequence, however, this one refuses to stay put. It is asserted in the first half of the passage only to be submerged in the stronger assertion of God's omnipresence; but it is revived in the second half of the passage as part of a succession of supersedures, each one undermining the basis of its predecessor. At one moment, the opposition is the obligatory one between the material and the spiritual; in the next, it is between the temple of the single heart, and the temple of all the hearts united (builded) together; and finally it is between a temporal temple of any size or shape, and a temple that stands and has always stood in Heaven. Although these oppositions follow one another in an order, that order seems reversible and permutable in any direction. (For example, the temporal temple would be emphasized over the eternal if one wanted to urge continued struggling in order to become a living stone.) One feels that any arrangement would be permitted except for one that would too narrowly construe templehood by insisting on the priority of one of its forms. The vocabulary may necessarily be one of means and end, struggle and goal, process and product, but because the argument into which it is structured is discontinuous, or multiply continuous, that same vocabulary is continually undermining the very fixities it momentarily establishes. Thus it is that we can have, in Hall's conclusion, temple praying to temple to be made into a temple:

Behold, if Solomon built a temple unto thee, thou hast built a temple unto thyself, in us. We are not only, through thy grace, living stones in thy temple, but living temples in thy Sion. Oh do thou ever dwell in this thy house; and in this thy house, let us ever serve thee.

The final section of this prayer—"and in this thy house, let us ever serve thee"—is invulnerable to paraphrase or parsing because by the time we reach it, it is impossible to separate out its constituents: "this house" can be either a material temple, or a single body, or the body of Christ ("in him we live and move and have our being"); "us" can refer either to those who would be living stones or to those who are already living stones, or to those who are living temples (not parts but wholes), and in fact refers to all those (the conjunction should be the additive "and" rather than the disjunctive "or"); where identity and difference are not maintained, the verb "serve" has no space to operate in; and "thee" implies a distance be-

tween petitioner and petitioned that is precisely what the
prayer, in its force, would remove.

All this applies equally to the text with which this chapter began, the prayer John Mayer places before his catechism, a text to whose resonances we can now respond
because we have been glossing it:

Thou which art the Master-builder of thine owne house, settle
me as one of thy living stones upon the right foundation, Jesus
Christ; in whom I may daily grow up, till that all the building
coupled together, groweth into an holy Temple in the Lord.

Everything that has been documented in the preceding
pages is concentrated here: the petition is that something
be done ("settle me as one of thy living stones"), but the
end of the prayer ("an holy Temple *in the Lord*") suggests
that it has been done already; Jesus Christ is at first the
foundation of a (projected) building, but then he turns
out to be identical with a building that already stands; we
begin with a metaphor of construction and the possibility
of failure; we end with the metaphor of growth and a
success that is assured from the beginning. It is also significant that the petitioner, in this case the catechist, is
asking to be made into a temple as he sets out to make
temples of his pupils. As it is in the commentaries, so is it
in the material prefatory to catechisms: there are temples
everywhere and they are at once distinguishable and interchangeable. The catechist is a temple (a vessel of the
Lord). The catechized are temples; they are, says Bishop
Jewel, "the temples and tabernacles of the Holy Ghost;
let us . . . bring them up in knowledge. . . . So shall
they be confirmed . . . and will grow unto perfect age in
Christ."[23] The catechism itself is a temple: Andrewes be-

23. *The Works of John Jewel, D.D. Bishop of Salisbury*, vol. VIII (Oxford,
1848), p. 51.

gins by likening "the course of Religion which we are to treat of . . . to a building," and Thomas Becon ends with the same comparison: "The doctrine, that thou hast now in the declaration of the Catechism uttered unto me, is in all points . . . grounded upon 'the foundation of the apostles and prophets, Jesus Christ himself being the head corner-stone.'"[24] Finally, and most obviously, catechizing, at least of the public kind, takes place in a temple, and all catechizing, whether public or private, has as its model, or its foundation, Jesus Christ, who reminds his betrayers, "I sat daily with you teaching in the temple" (Matthew 26:55), a text, we are told, that orders the life of Herbert's parson (pp. 227–228).

Even when the word "temple" is not used by a catechist, his deployment of the "building" metaphor will reach out to it, for that metaphor has its source in the temple-texts and shares with them a parallel set of distinguishable yet equivalent structures. At the beginning of John Frewen's catechism, it is the individual believer who is being edified or built up: "in whomsoever these Doctrines . . . are not settled . . . there is absolutely no more stableness in the Christianity of such a one . . . then of a building without a good foundation" (pp. 5–6). In the paragraphs that follow, the foundation broadens to support a structure of whole families ("their dwelling places . . . should be as so many little Churches"), and Frewen concludes with a vision of the entire community united by catechizing to form an assembly of saints (the Church Militant) that will eventually triumph in Heaven, "builded up from one degree of holinesse to another, even untill we become members of Jesus Christ, and enjoy eternall life" (p. 17). In this, its

24. *The Catechism of Thomas Becon* (Cambridge, 1844), p. 409.

final appearance, the "building" metaphor is complicated in ways that forge still another link with the
temple-commentaries. The spiritual "building up" to
which the image of a physical building has stood as (dis-
posable) vehicle to tenor, is now revealed to have as *its*
goal absorption (or disappearance) into yet another
building, one that is both physical and spiritual, the
body, incarnate and mystical, of Jesus Christ. Moreover,
"goal" is precisely the wrong word (although Frewen's
rhetoric supports it) because the "degrees" or steps do
not produce the perfect structure which is, in fact, the
producer of *them*: Jesus Christ is the foundation, the
master-builder, and the building, the material, efficient,
and final cause. Like every other catechist, Frewen must
watch his building rise into a life he did not infuse. At the
heart of catechistical rhetoric is the same paradox that can
be read out of the phrase "temple of God": the great work
to which catechists and their charges are exhorted—the
raising of a holy building—has already been accomplished.

If catechistical rhetoric and the rhetoric of temple building share a metaphor they also share its negative pole. In
both literatures, the alternative to being the temple of
God is to be instead the chapel of the devil. Immediately
after characterizing those who are to be catechized as
"the temples and tabernacle of the Holy Ghost," Bishop
Jewel warns, "let us not suffer the foul spirit to possess
them, and dwell within them." Richard Preston declares
that "wheresoever God buildeth his Church, there the
Divell buildeth his Chappell," and his "wheresoever"
includes not only buildings, but communities and individuals: "For as God began to build his Church in righte-
ous *Abell*, so likewise the divell began to build his Chap-

pell in wicked *Caine* . . . and as God in these our dayes
doth build his Church, in Christian Princes, vertuous rul-
ers, holy and reverend Church Governors, learned writers and zealous Preachers . . . so the divell ceaseth not to
build his Chappell in the Papists."[25] Anthony Burgesse's commentary on I Cor. 3:16—"Know ye not that
ye are the temple of God, and that the spirit of God
dwelleth in you?"—reminds us of a state in which we
were not temples at all: "We . . . once were the Devils, he
dwelt in us, *He ruleth in the hearts of the disobedient.*"[26]
These disobedient, says Paul Baynes, "are the devills
Chappell, rather than God's temple," and he asks rhe-
torically, "can these filthinesses have aboad in a temple of
God? . . . Can these be in Christ, in whom, whosoever is
builded by Faith, must grow to bee a holy temple of the
Lord? No, surely."[27] Of these four statements, two are
from catechisms and two from commentaries on the
word "temple"; the contexts are perfectly congruent and
the components they share are interchangeable.

3. TEMPLES IN *THE TEMPLE*

We are now in a position to list these components and so
to fill out a rhetoric of templehood. The first component is
a vocabulary: it includes stones, foundations, builders,
buildings, houses, hearts, and, of course, temples. This
vocabulary is deployed in such a way as to raise a series of

25. Richard Preston, *The Doctrine of the Sacrament of the Lords Supper
handled* (1621), sigs. A2^v–A3^r.

26. *The Scripture directory*, p. 205. See also p. 228: "Do not thou then
judge of thy self, as the Temple of God, when thou art like a dung-hill;
thy heart is not a sacred Temple, but an open Inne or Marketplace; all
strange lusts may lodge in thee."

27. *A commentary upon the epistle*, p. 331.

questions concerning the field of reference it supposedly
picks out: these are questions of agency (who is doing
what to whom?), of sequence (has something already
been done, or is it about to be done, or is it even now
being done?), of the status of phenomenal objects (are we
talking about a physical structure, a community, a heart,
a soul, a body?) and of the nature of action (is it progressive or intermittent, determined or accidental, organic or
mechanical?). These questions are in turn in the service of
a set of related strategies: the merely material or visible is
de-emphasized in favor of the spiritual, the outer in favor
of the inner; the desire to arrange objects and events in an
intelligible order, which could presumably be repeated,
is frustrated; and the distinctions that are unavoidably
established by the very act of predication (between persons, things, and states) are continually undermined.

If this characterization fits both the material prefatory
to catechisms and the commentaries on the constellation
of temple texts, it does no less well for Herbert's poetry.
For example, the preceding paragraph could well be a
description of Herbert's "The Church-floore": the poem
begins as a meditation on the floor or foundation which is
joined, as the perspective widens, by door, room, heart,
and builder. These objects are first distinguished (from
each other and from the reader) and then brought together, as the architectural metaphor becomes alive and
is finally interiorized. The strategy is to de-emphasize the
material in favor of the spiritual by disallowing the phenomenal distinctions the verse at first encourages (between the Church, the speaker, his heart, and the heart
of the reader), and the strategy succeeds when the reader
is no longer trying to make these distinctions, but discovers himself signified by each and every one of them (he

discovers what he is). It is then, as the poem formally closes down, that it truly opens up, reaching out to the very texts whose network of interrelationships is the substance of catechetical rhetoric. Indeed, a passage from T. W.'s praise of catechizing could serve as this poem's gloss:

As from buildings wher the foundation or groundworke useth first to be laid, that the walles and roofs may be reared and raised upon it: Even so in the spiritual building up of mens consciences to God, the doctrine of Catechisme is first to be laid as a foundation, and afterward the misterie of Christ is more highly and deeply to bee handled, as it were the rearing of the walles, roofe, and loover.[28]

Nor is "The Church-floore" unique in *The Temple*. The poem that follows it, "The Windows," displays the same components and exhibits the same strategies. It begins with a question:

Lord, how can man preach thy eternall word?

The question, as in many of Herbert's poems, assumes (and therefore establishes) the distinctions it will finally collapse, in this case the distinctions between the speaker (standing in for the generic "man"), his God, and the "eternall word." The issue is the fitness of man to be a preacher (in other poems it will be the fitness of his heart to be a temple). He is manifestly *un*fit—"He is a brittle crazie glasse"—and his unfitness only serves to magnify the grace God displays in allowing him to serve:

Yet in thy temple thou dost him afford
This glorious and transcendent place,
To be a window, through thy grace.
(lines 3–5)

28. *An exposition*, p. 2.

As we read this first stanza, its final line may feel anticlimactic because it does not live up to the promise of the line before it: being a window may be above man's deserts, but it would seem less than a "glorious and transcendent place." The action of these lines is to diminish man even further, and the agency of that diminishing is the word "place," which is ambiguous between "physical location" and "position or status." The first sense seems to be the primary one at the end of line 4 which, for a moment, is read as marking the completion of a thought: although he is undeserving, man has been afforded a large and important space in God's temple. Indeed, it is possible to read the lines so that the space is the temple itself; "in thy temple" would then mean "in the form or fact of thy temple" and be in apposition to "This glorious and transcendent place." In line 5, however, we discover that the thought is not complete and that "place" (along with the phrase it concludes) now stands in apposition to "To be a window." Immediately, "place" is understood to signify "position in the sense of status," and this new understanding acts out the judgmental content the word now has. That is, by replacing one sense of "place" with another, we demote man; he is no longer a proprietor of the temple or of some large portion of it; he is merely one of its furnishings. In short, we put him in his place, in both senses; he has a place in the place, and it is distinctly subordinate.

The reader, of course, labors less over these lines than I have. The adjustment he makes is easy and unselfconscious; but simply by making it, he adds another distinction to those established in the opening lines, a distinction between man and the temple in which he is allowed

a place. As we proceed to the second stanza that distinction is at first reinforced:

> But when thou dost anneal in glasse thy storie,
>   Making thy life to shine within.
>
> (lines 6–7)

This would seem to make clearer man's role as a window
in the temple: it is through him that God's light (or life)
shines on its way in. That is, "within" is read as "on the
other side of"; it maintains the discreteness of the window and the glorious and transcendent place on which it
opens. But line 8 reveals that the object of the adverb is
the holy preacher ("to shine within / The holy Preachers")
and suddenly "within" must be reinterpreted as "inside
of." Rather than mediating between God and his temple,
the preacher is now understood to *be* that temple, made
so by the life that shines within him. Again we must
make a small adjustment, and by making it we participate
in the growth of the preacher (only six lines ago such
unpromising material) into the temple of God, and we do
this by removing the distance between them, a distance
we had ourselves established in the previous stanzas.
The sequence of interpretive acts is the same we perform
while reading "Love-joy" and "Jesu": an initial misreading when it seems that the preacher is to be given the
temple (is afforded this glorious and transcendent place),
a corrected reading that firmly separates them, and a final
reading that brings them together again, but in a relationship not merely of contiguity, but of identity, for "Know
ye not that ye are the temple of God, and that the spirit of
God dwelleth in you?"

   If this key text is one to which "The Windows" asks us

to reach out (it is the deep and dark point of religion to which we are driven), it is the text that stands behind every line of "Sion";

> Lord, with what glorie wast thou serv'd of old,
> When Solomons temple stood and flourished!
>> Where most things were of purest gold;
>> The wood was all embellished
> With flowers and carvings, mysticall and rare:
> All show'd the builders, crav'd the seers care.
>> (lines 1–6)

The lament for the passing of former glories is a satiric convention in which the opposition between old and new is an opposition between original virtue and its decline; but in the context of "temple" rhetoric the values of old and new are reversed (the old law is oppressive and external, the new liberating and inner) and the reader cannot help but supply a counterpoint to the poem's assertion. As a result, the qualifying "Yet" which begins the second stanza is no surprise; it has been anticipated along with the contrastive statement it introduces:

> Yet all this glorie, all this pomp and state
> Did not affect thee much, was not thy aim;
>> Something there was, that sow'd debate:
>> Wherfore thou quitt'st thy ancient claim:
> And now thy Architecture meets with sinne;
> For all thy frame and fabrick is within.
>> (lines 7–12)

The two arguments of the poem meet in the rhyme of "sinne" and "within." The first completes the statement begun in the opening stanza: where once you were worshipped in buildings of purest gold and embellished wood, now your temple is less substantial and is vulnerable to sin. The second completes the movement begun by "yet": all these trappings were external; your real con-

cern is with what is happening within. By joining the
words in a rhyme, Herbert yokes together the forces that
pull against one another in his poem. The result is a moment of poised tension and the creation of a pressure that
is eased and released when, in the final two stanzas,
"sinne" and "within" are revealed to be not antagonistic
but necessary to one another:

> There thou art struggling with a peevish heart,
> Which sometimes crosseth thee, thou sometimes it:
> > The fight is hard on either part.
> > Great God doth fight, he doth submit.
> All Solomons sea of brasse and world of stone
> Is not so deare to thee as one good grone.
>
> > > (lines 13–18)

> And truly brasse and stones are heavie things,
> Tombes for the dead, not temples fit for thee:
> > But grones are quick and full of wings,
> > And all their motions upward be;
> And ever as they mount, like larks they sing;
> The note is sad, yet musick for a King.
>
> > > (lines 19–24)

Without sin, the inner structure will not rise, for its materials are the groans wrung from the heart by the struggles
within it. The institution of the poem's new values is fully
achieved when the very substantiality of Solomon's temple becomes the reason for its unfitness. The stones that
are too heavy are replaced by the "livelie stones" which
as Ryley says are not "mute, & passive" but "Active on
their motion God, & Heaven ward" (p. 347); and the
temple itself is replaced by the heart. Ryley's commentary makes all these points and documents the poem's
position in the tradition we have been tracing:

They [the gold and wood of the material temple] Served but as
Shaddows of Good things to Come: &, w^n y^t Substance was
come, these Shaddows were done away. *he quit his claim* to this

pompous Temple, & builds one *within*, y^t is in ye heart of man; *Solomon built him a house, how be it ye most high dwelleth not in Temples made with hands. Ye are ye Temple of God. Act: 7.27.28. I Cor. 3.16* & see it analogized in y^e *(Church Floor).* (p. 347).

By sending us from "Sion" to "The Churche-floore" Ryley anticipates and gives support to the thesis of these pages: *The Temple* is not only the title of this collection, it identifies the metaphor that informs and relates the poems within it. "Sion" is merely the poem that most fully presents the components of that metaphor; like Ryley, we can move out from it to many of the others. The issue raised in line 20—what distinguishes "Tombes for the dead" from "temples fit for thee"—has a poem of its own, "Sepulchre":

> O Blessed Bodie! Whither art thou thrown?
> No lodging for thee, but a cold hard stone?
> So many hearts on earth, and yet not one
>   Receive thee?

As one might predict in the light of the tradition we have been following, the poem will proceed by bringing together the two objects—stone and heart—whose distinctness this first stanza assumes. That assumption runs counter to the knowledge possessed by the reader who is thus in the familiar Herbertian position of supplying answers to a question that has only indirectly been asked (he is being driven by means of what he knows to "that which he knows not"). The question is "where can we find a place for the body of Christ, since so many of the hearts on earth are so stony?" The answer is that these same hearts have been made fit—they are not hard, but lively stones—by the very person who already occupies them, who has made them into living temples by writing his law "not in tables of stone, but in fleshly tables of the heart." This answer is not given in the poem; rather it must be supplied by a reader who is responding to its deliberately (and provocatively) narrow assertions. Every line of the poem works as the promptings of Herbert's parson work, by driving the reader to articulate for himself a deep and dark point of religion.[29]

That deep and dark point is always the same: Christ is everywhere and doing all things. What he is doing in many of these poems is building temples. In "Man" the temple is already built and it appears that the only question is whether or not God will dwell in it:

> My God, I heard this day,
> That none doth build a stately habitation,
> But he that means to dwell therein.
> What house more stately hath there been,
> Or can be, then is Man? to whose creation
> All things are in decay.
>
> (lines 1–6)

Like so many of Herbert's poems this one leads a double life, it has a "double motion" ("Coloss. 3.3.," line 2). It takes the overt form of an extended praise, but that praise is merely a strategy made necessary by the absence of the very qualities it rehearses. The object of praise is man, who is represented in stanzas 2 through 8 as the perfect structure, free standing, stable, proportioned, unified, whole:

> For Man is ev'ry thing (line 7)
> Man is all symmetrie,
> Full of proportions   (lines 13–14)
> For us the windes do blow   (line 25)

29. See *Self-Consuming Artifacts*, pp. 174–176.

> The starres have us to bed   (line 31)
> More servants wait on Man,
> Then he'l take notice of   (lines 43, 44)

In the last stanza, however, the true purpose of this praise is revealed: it is a ploy designed to attract the one person whose presence in the building will make what has been asserted of it true:

> Since then, my God, thou hast
> So brave a Palace built; O dwell in it,
> That it may dwell with thee at last!
> Till then, afford us so much wit;
> That, as the world serves us, we may serve thee,
> And both thy servants be.
>
>   (lines 49–54)

Only when God dwells in the temple will it be a temple. Until then it is a structure that lacks everything the speaker claims for it. The poem pursues a double strategy: it invites God to make those claims good, and at the same time it invites the reader to take them literally.[30] If he accepts the invitation (and the possibility is increased by the shift in stanza 5 from "man" to "us" as the object of praise), he will be claiming for himself the very perfections that only God's presence can confer, and the revelation of the final stanza will be a rebuke to his presumption. He will join with the speaker in a prayer he might have uttered before ("O dwell in it"), but he now utters it with a new (because personal) knowledge of how important it is that God answer it. Once again, the reader of a Herbert poem is brought by means of that which he knows (that he is a temple of God) to that which he

30. See the quite different interpretations in Martz, *Poetry of Meditation*, pp. 59–61, Rickey, *Utmost Art*, pp. 143–144, and Arnold Stein, *George Herbert's Lyrics* (Baltimore, 1968), pp. 101–103.

knows not or at least has momentarily forgotten (that his status as a temple depends entirely on God's making him so). The sequence here is both like and unlike that of "Sepulchre." In one poem the reader supplies what the speaker has provokingly omitted; he corrects the speaker. In the other, the reader is corrected when he fails to discern the speaker's true intention (to use self-praise as a strategy). In both poems, however, the reader participates in his own edification, discovering, as the pupils of Herbert's parson discover, what he is (the temple of God).

The analyses of the preceding pages make two related and interdependent points: first, viewed as strategies, Herbert's poems are consistently answerable to his description of the parson catechizing, and second, they do their work in the context of the metaphor that more than any other is associated with catechistical practice and its effects. In the sequence of "The Church" that metaphor takes as many forms as there are structures that can be presented as discrete and independent—churches, houses, palaces, rooms, hearts, sepulchres, boxes, poems, lines, verses, frames, windows, floors, altars, days, months, minutes, hours, minerals, plants, stars, professions (priests, poets), courts, individual men, families, nations, the world. Inevitably, in the course of a poem these structures lose their discreteness precisely because they are revealed to be dependent on the same informing and sustaining spirit that makes of all of them what the poem—like the efforts of Herbert's parson—is making of the reader, a temple of God. This process takes place not only within poems, but between them. Ryley's headnote to "Man" tells us that "This poem . . . is much ye Same, for ye Subject of it, as that Called ye world" (p.

279). That poem begins "Love built a stately house" and rehearses a cycle of decay and rebuilding which ends with the house once again firmly established: "But *Love* and *Grace* took *Glorie* by the hand,/ And built a braver palace then before." As Ryley observes, the subject of the poem could be *either* "ye world we live in" or "the State Man" (p. 254). It is, of course, both, because both are supported by Grace and informed by Love. The smaller world and the greater alike are temples of God, and without his active presence they are equally vulnerable to the assaults of Sin and Death who together try "To raze the building to the very floore" (line 17). The building they raze could very well be the church-heart of "The Churche-floore" and the floor they leave is the foundation on which the apostles and their successors, the catechizers, raise up a succession of living temples. Ryley's perception of a homology between "The World" and "Man" can be extended to every one of the poems we have examined and to many more. Indeed, by my count, no less than sixty-two poems in the sequence can be directly related to the temple topos (and these sixty-two are spaced so that there are never more than three poems in succession without such a direct relationship), a statistic that gives body to Daniel Baker's praise of "mighty *Herbert*, who upon the Place/ A Temple built, that does outgo /Both *Solomon's*, and *Herod's* too,/ And all the Temples of the Gods by far."[31]

Here the several strains of our argument begin to converge. It has been demonstrated that (1) there is a commonplace association between catechizing and temple-building, that (2) Herbert was aware of this association

31. Ray, p. 314.

and thought seriously enough about it to develop a theory of catechizing quite distinctive from that of his contemporaries, that (3) the components of the metaphor that link the two activities—the metaphor of the building—are found everywhere in Herbert's poems, that (4) viewed as strategies, these same poems are precisely answerable to the description in *A Priest To the Temple* and of the parson catechizing, and that (5) in their response to him, the men and women of Herbert's century would seem to provide further support for a characterization of his poetry as catechistical. The evidence, however, is still inconclusive, and paradoxically, it is inconclusive because there is too much of it. That is to say, the "temple-building" metaphor is so pervasive, so much a staple of Christian rhetoric in its every form, that one cannot really argue from its appearance in one homiletic mode to the direct influence of another; indeed, its absence would be a fact of greater inferential significance. What I have been able to show, I think, is that in the seventeenth century when one thinks of catechisms one thinks immediately of temples; but what I have yet to show is that when one thinks of this particular temple—a body of religious verse—one should think of catechisms. I believe that I can show that and therefore offer a persuasive case for the large assertion of this study, that *The Temple* was composed on a catechistical model.

Three: The Children Of The Precept: Catechizing And The Liturgy

1. THE SEQUENCE OF THE EXTENDED CATECHUMENATE

THE FINAL piece of evidence is to be found once again in the prefaces to Reformation catechisms. In 1580, W. Charcke penned an introduction to his translation into Latin of "A Catechisme for the Frenche Churche" by Robert Masson Fontaine. The introduction bears the familiar title, "Of the use of Catechising," and in it Charcke rehearses the standard arguments and employs the obligatory topoi. He begins with the topos of the foundations. In the building of the house of God, a builder must take "greatest care . . . that hee make not the walles, or set up the house, before he have well laide the foundations, without the which to hasten to the other worke, is altogether in vaine" (sigs. C8ᵛ–D1ʳ). The foundations are immediately identified with "the Catechisme," and the identification is supported by citations from the usual texts, I Corinthians 3, I Peter 2, and Hebrews 5. In the paragraphs that follow, Charcke's emphasis falls on the importance of the right order in instruction: "so needful a thing it is in al religions, as in other artes in the beginning, often to beate in the first groundes, and afterwards in method & order to ope other things" (sig. D3ʳ). Men who do not learn the first principles will confess their faith without understanding: "in wordes they boldly say [presumably at their confirmation], they hope for the thing, which by no sharpnes of wit, they do conceave" (sig. D2ᵛ). Even worse, they are "haled to the holy supper . . . altogether ignorant of the maiestie & dignities of so high a mysterie," and, as a result, "in steed of the foode of the soul, they receive the poyson of the soule; and in the place of everlasting salvation, get everlasting condemnation" (sig. D3ᵛ). As a protection against these dangers (and a host of others) Charcke repeatedly urges the "expounding of the Catechisme," and he brings his exhortation to a close by elaborating two similitudes, one alimentary, the other architectural:

Doubtless, they which as it were in their swadling clouts have any time tasted the most sweete meate of milke, and most easie to digest, afterwardes at the table it selfe shall receive stronger meate of a stronger disposition, to strengthen the power & senses of the body: that is, they which as it were in the Porche of the temple, doe learne out of Catechismes the first groundes of religion, afterwardes, being let in as it were into the Sanctuary, shall much more calmly and pleasantly enter into the last & deepest mysteries of our redemption and sanctification. (sigs. D4ʳ⁻ᵛ)

One is struck immediately by the parallel between this last formulation and the main divisions of *The Temple*; and a context for that parallel is provided by another passage from the same volume. The author is John Stockwood, schoolmaster of Tunbridge, who writes an

"Epistle Dedicatorie" to the collection in which Charcke's introduction appears, along with other treatises concerning the use and profit of catechizing.[1] Stockwood is addressing "the right worshipfull and godly Lady, the Lady Golding," and urging her, as we might expect, to continue in the practice of catechizing her family and servants. "Goe on," he says,

> in the good way which you have begunne, and continue foorth the laudable race, that heeretofore you have runne, in the providing for the diligent instruction of your house and family in the knowledge of God and principles of Christian religion, which duetie in the first & best times of the primitive Churche was thought to be so necessary & needful, that they had those which of purpose attended on this office, yea & so streight was the Discipline of that age, that they suffered not those that were not yet gone past the A B C of Christianitie, or the doctrin of the beginning of Christ (as it is tearmed in the Hebrewes by the Apostle) to come once within the Churche, but kept them aloofe without, in a place by themselves, as it might bee now with us the Church Porche. (printers device, 6^{r-v})

Stockwood's commentary allows us to see that Charcke is not merely reaching for a metaphor when he compares the progress of catechistical instruction to the stages by which one might move from the porch of a Church into its sanctuary. Rather he is referring to a tradition that would have been familiar both to the writers and readers of catechisms, a tradition he cites precisely because of the authority given by Protestant polemicists to the practices of "the primitive Churche." In T. W.'s catechism, the Questioner asks *"How may the antiquitie of this manner of teaching be collected?"* The Answerer responds,

1. *A shorte and fruitefull treatise, of the profite and necessitie of Catechising: That is, of instructing the youth, and ignorant persons in the principles and groundes of Christian religion* (London, 1580).

"Thus. It could be no new thing but very auncient being used in the time of the primitive Church, even so far off as in the age and time of the Apostles. And that it was used in those times is plaine . . . *by 1 Cor. 3.*"[2] Becon's catechism is even more emphatic on the point. To the Father's query, "Is not this kind of teaching younglings new, and lately invented?" the Son responds "No, verily," and he goes on to give a brief outline of its history:

In the primitive church there were not only bishops and pastors that preached the gospel of Christ to the people, which were already grafted by baptism and the Holy Ghost in Christ Jesu, but also certain teachers called *catechistae*, which taught not only the young children that were already baptized, but also such as being in age came and were contented to forsake gentility and to take upon them Christianity, . . . the principles of Christian religion, before they received baptism and were openly admitted into the congregation of the faithful. And as these teachers were called *catechistae*, that is to say, instructors, or teachers; so likewise were the younglings called *catechumini*, that is to say, persons instructed or taught. And the office of the catechist was not only to instruct and teach, but also to examine such as they taught how they profited and increased in the knowledge of God's mysteries; and if they failed at any point, diligently to instruct and teach them, till they were exercised in the doctrine of Christ.[3]

Again Becon's (relative) expansiveness allows us to become more sensitive readers of Charcke's tantalizingly brief statement. It is clear that Charcke's "temporal" vocabulary—words and phrases like "first," "afterwardes," "shall enter," "last"—has reference not only to the stages in a course of instruction, but also to the stages by which one becomes a member of a community. The

2. *An exposition*, pp. 3–4.
3. *The Catechism of Thomas Becon*, p. 9.

stages are three: a period of instruction before baptism, an examination directly preceding baptism (or confirmation if the pupils were Christians baptized as infants), and a period of post-baptismal instruction as the newly initiated are admitted to the sacraments, "the last and deepest mysteries of our redemption & sanctification." It is in this sequence, says Henry Holland, that "in elder ages the babes in Christ were carefully taught the first grounds of Religion: and so being well grounded they were admitted by confirmation and laying on of hands to the Lords Supper."[4] "Babes in Christ" is obviously ambiguous: it refers both to those who were actually babes, young Christian children being nourished by the milk of the pure word, and those who, while they might be fully grown and superbly educated, were nonetheless infants in the knowledge of a religion that asked for a radical devaluation of everything they knew and held dear. J. F[otherby] makes the distinction clear and also makes clear its importance:

Ecclesiastical Writers make mention of two manners of catechizing, which differed both in regard of time, and in respect of persons: the one was before Baptisme, the other was after Baptisme; the one was catechizing of them that were strangers from the Covenant; the other was of them that were in the Covenant: the one was of the heathens, before they were received into Gods Covenant, and into the fellowship of the Church: the other was of the children of the faithfull.[5]

Instruction of the children of the faithful, leading to an examination at which they were "to render a reason of their faith . . . in the presence of the Congregation"

4. *The historie of Adam or the foure-fold State of Man,* sig. A3ʳ.
5. *The covenant betweene God and Man. Playnely declared, in laying open the cheifest points of Christian Religion* (1616), pp. 59–60.

(p. 63) is, of course, confirmation, as it is retained in the Anglican liturgy; it is administered to those who have always been *in* the Church. The instruction of the heathens is, in one way, of more consequence, since any failure to pass the examination will debar them from entering the Church, both in the sense that they will not be admitted into the community (a mystical body) and in the sense that they will not be allowed to pass through the Church's doors; they will be stopped, literally, at the church porch. ("They suffered not those that were not yet gone past the A B C of Christianitie . . . to come once within the Churche.") It was because so much was at stake, especially for a new Church that was concerned to protect its purity against the defilement of an alien majority, that the initiatory rites were elaborate and the period of preparation long:

. . . if any heathen man desired to be received into the fellowship of the Church, he was first catechised in the principles of Religion, and then hearing further the Word of God . . . afterward came into the face of the Congregation, and confessed that hee did believe . . . whereupon he was baptized, and received into the fellowship of the Church. . . . And that this order might bee the better observed, the Church appointed certaine times, and in some places a longer space, at other times, and in other places a shorter time, for catechising of Heathens, before they were baptized. *Socrates*, lib. 7 cap. 30 writeth, that the Burgonians were seven dayes in learning their catechisme, and then baptized the eight, *Jerome, ad Pammachium* saith, the custome in his dayes, was to catechise them fourty days, and then to baptize them. *Tertullian de baptismo*, writeth that there were two times in the year, Easter and Whitsontide, specially appointed by the Church for Baptisme, and strangers from the Covenant were instructed in the principles of Religion, all the rest of the yeare, against these two times. (pp. 60–61)

In fact, the period of instruction could be as long as three years; [6] what is important, however, is not the accuracy of these accounts, but the fact that they are found in so many shapes and sizes; for this indicates that the picture of things they are presenting is, at least in its general outlines, a familiar and conventional one. It is also detailed. Even the briefest of commentaries will sketch out the three catechistical stages, and refer to one or more Fathers as a source. Hooker cites Tertullian, Cyprian, and Rupert in the margin of his paragraph, and in a single sentence he manages to communicate a sense of the sequence, suggest its relationship both to the receiving of the sacraments and to the entry into the physical church, and introduce one of its special terms:

> Such as were trained up in these rudiments, and were so made fit to be afterwardes by Baptisme received into the Church, the Fathers usually in their writings do tearme *Hearers*, as having no farther communion or fellowship with the Church then only this, that they were admitted to heare the principles of Christian faith made plaine unto them. [7]

Immanuel Bourne is as prolix as Hooker is concise. In his catechism, *A light from Christ*, the history of the early catechumenate is rehearsed twice. In *The Epistle Dedicatory* (addressed to the Parliament) Bourne traces the practice of catechizing from "faithful *Abraham*" to "the Primitives times" when "the Church was exceeding vigilant for this duty." [8] The Church, he declares, "had their Catechists or Catechizers," and he names St. Cyprian, Pantenus, Origen, Clemens Alexandrinus, Jerome, and

6. See J. A. Jungmann, *The Early Liturgy* (Notre Dame, 1969), p. 77.

7. *Of The Lawes of Ecclesiasticall Politie, The Fift Booke* (1579), p. 29.

8. Immanuel Bourne, *A light from Christ, leading unto Christ, by the star of his word* (1646), sig. A1[r].

Cyril of Jerusalem. To this list he adds some "late learned Writers, Mr. *Calvin, Musculus, Peter Martyr, Ursinus, Bucanus, Beza, Danaeus, Zanchius, Alstedius,* Mr. *Virel.* Our English, Mr. *Nowel,* Mr. *Perkins,* Mr. *Egerton,* Mr. *Dod,* Mr. *Baal,* Mr. *Downame,* Mr. *Allen,* Mr. *Twisse,* Dr. *Maier,* and many other laborious workmen in the Lords Vineyard" (sig. a2ʳ). Clearly, Bourne sees himself the inheritor of a long tradition, and in the body of his catechism he explores its origins at length. The context is a complaint against those who are merely outward professors. It was precisely to protect the Church from such men and women, Bourne explains, that the catechumenate was instituted, for "the Saints did not presently then upon the first seeming conversion, or profession of themselves to believe, admit men or women so much as to Baptisme, much lesse to the Sacrament of the Lords Supper; but had a time of tryall and preparation for so great a work: Therefore Writers relate there were severall orders of Christians in the Church of Christ" (p.9). Bourne's account of these "severall orders" is very full. First there were those who were candidates for becoming candidates for baptism, "*Catechumens,* hearers, and learners of the Doctrine of the Gospel by Catechizing . . . yea, though they were men of ripe years, untill they were able to make a good profession of their Faith, and give evidence of their sincere conversion and resolution" (p. 9). Among those who submitted to this trial and preparation were Arnobius, Ambrose, and Augustine. The second order "were such Catechumens or Catechized persons, who, when they were well tryed and proved, or examined and approved, came to desire Baptisme, and were called Competitors, or Fellow-Catechumens desiring Baptisme, which when they received, they were arrayed

in white robes'' (pp. 10–11). Those who were thus baptized and arrayed became members of a third order:

They were called the Faithfull; and these were such Believers,
or Beleeving Christians, who after they were baptized, & had
made profession & proof of their faith, were admitted to the
Lords Table, and had communion with their fellow-Saints in
that holy Ordinance and so were all fellow members of the
mysticall Body of Christ. And in the first Primitive times of the
Apostles and Church after Christ, these Believers were together, and were of one heart, and of one soul; a sweet example
of unity for the Churches of Christ to the end of the world.
(p. 11)

Thus what begins as a course of instruction for those
outside the Church (in both the spiritual and physical
sense) ends in a vision of the last things; but lest his
readers receive that vision complacently, Bourne immediately reminds them of a fourth order,

The Penitents, (who were such believers) as after profession of
their Faith, and partaking of the Sacrament, did fall into some
open, notorious, scandalous sin, and were put back into the
number and place of the Catechumens, and kept from the Sacrament, untill upon true signes of Repentance, and satisfaction
to the Church, they were received again into their former order,
and re-admitted unto the Lord's Supper. (pp. 11–12)

Or, in other words, they were turned away from the altar
and put back in the company of those who were still
receiving instruction on the church porch.

It remains only for Bourne to relate the sequence of the
extended catechumenate to the liturgy of his own day.
The chief difference, of course, is the change from a procedure ending in conversion to one in which instruction
is given to those who were baptized at birth. The Questioner puts the issue directly: "*Thus you have shewed the*

practice of the Church for men of ripe years converted to the Faith, and for such as were Communicants once received: But what say you of Children of believing Parents, born in the Church, and received by Baptisme, as outward visible members of the Church?" (pp. 12–13). The answer is that these too are "without doubt . . . to be catechized and instructed in the knowledge of God, and of themselves, and of Christ, and of the Sacrament, & be able to make profession of their Faith, before they be admitted to the Lords Table" (p. 11). That is, in a society already Christian, communion tends to replace baptism as the focus and goal of catechistical instruction. For Bourne and others, however, this only increases its importance, and he ends this section by declaring roundly that "Catechizing is a necessary duty in the Church of Christ" (p. 14).

There is a massive body of scholarship on the subject of the catechumenate as it relates to early liturgical practices. What is surprising is how little our knowledge has advanced beyond the summary accounts given by catechists like Bourne.[9] In general, modern scholars concern themselves with the details of a picture whose outlines they do not challenge. They debate the differences between the Eastern and Roman rites, the relationship between baptism and confirmation, the precise number of degrees and orders in the catechumenate, the length of the various stages, and so on; but one could take any number of positions on these issues and still subscribe to Jean Daniélou's recent description of the sequence:

From the third century on, the catechumens were a distinct order in the Church. They were subject to a time of trial in the

9. See also Jeremias Bastingius, *An exposition or commentarie upon the catechisme of Christian religion,* sigs. A3^v–A4^r, and *A Catechisme . . . By Alexander Nowell,* ed. G. E. Corrie, pp. 210–211.

course of which the aptitude of each candidate to lead a Christian life was scrutinized and the strength of his faith was examined. We can distinguish two stages each of which was inaugurated by an examination: (1) a rather prolonged period preliminary to the receiving of Baptism; during this time the candidates were called *catechoumenoi* in the East, *audientes* in the West. (2) the period immediately preparatory for Baptism; during this time the candidates were called *photizomenoi* in the East and *electi* in the West. After their baptism, the new Christians were required to complete their initiation in the course of a third stage, briefer than the other two because it was limited to Easter week, but nonetheless very important. It was during these few days that the mystagogical lectures revealed to them the full meaning of the sacrament they had come to receive. We have thus three major stations in the progress which brought the catechumen to the full bloom of the Christian life. Another station generally preceded them, at which the pagans informed themselves about the faith they had heard proclaimed and seen others practice. We know that many such came to Origen's lectures. In the west they were called *accedentes* and (by Augustine) *rudes*. [10]

Daniélou's basic sources are by and large those cited by Fotherby, Holland, Hooker, and others: Tertullian, Ambrose, Origen, Cyril, Augustine, Cyprian, Clement. He also has recourse to texts that have only recently been rediscovered (*The Apostolic Tradition* of Hippolytus, the *Journal* of Etheria, Irenaeus's *The Presentation of the Apostolic Preaching*) but for the most part these do not displace but supplement the documents that were available to the catechists of the sixteenth and seventeenth centuries. Indeed, in most respects the accounts of Daniélou and Bourne are interchangeable. They are both somewhat idealized descriptions of the catechumenate as it proba-

10. Jean Daniélou and Régine du Charlat, *La Catéchèse Aux Premiers Siècles* (Paris, 1968), p. 45. The translation is mine.

bly flourished in the third and fourth centuries, and therefore they fairly represent what the seventeenth century reader of *The Temple* would have known about the early liturgy and the rites of initiation.

That same reader would have seen that, like the sequence of Herbert's poetry, these rites are progressive, in two senses: the catechumens progress from a place outside the Church (or on its porch) to the baptistry, and from there to the altar before exiting from the Church to join the Church Militant; and the stages of their progress coincide with changes in the nature of the instruction they receive. The point is made explicitly by Cyril, when he concludes his *Procatechesis* with this warning:

These Catechetical lectures, addressed to candidates for Enlightenment, may be given to those going forward for Baptism and to the already baptized faithful. They may, on no account, be given to catechumens or to other classes of non-Christians.[11]

These "other classes," made up of those who were not yet admitted to formal candidacy, received another kind of instruction. It was, as J. A. Jungmann observes, not a systematic doctrinal instruction, but "a period of moral trial, a sort of novitiate with religious and ascetical exercises, together with suitable instructions; to become a Christian in those days was comparable to entering some strict order at the present time."[12] The strictness of the

11. *The Works of Saint Cyril,* vol. I, ed. L. P. McCauley, S. J. and A. A. Stephenson (Washington, 1970), pp. 84–85. For similar statements see *The Treatise on the Apostolic Tradition of St. Hippolytus of Rome,* ed. Rev. Gregory Dix (London, 1968), p. 43, and *Peregrinatio Etheriae,* in L. Duchesne, *Christian Worship: Its Origin and Evolution* (London, 1904), p. 574.

12. *The Early Liturgy,* p. 77.

order is apparent in Hippolytus's directions for the pro-
cessing of new converts: "Let them be examined as to the
reason why they have come forward to the faith. . . . Let
their life and manner of living be enquired into."[13] There
follows a list of interdicted activities and professions; if
an aspirant persisted in any of these, he or she was to be
"rejected" and "cast out." It is only after this initial
examination or scrutiny that the new catechumens are
allowed to "hear the word" (p. 28), that is, to begin the
three-year period of the catechumenate. Even then,
however, they are set apart, praying by themselves
rather than with the faithful, dismissed, along with the
penitents, after the prayers and sermon, but before the
service of the Eucharist. A second examination follows
the conclusion of this stage, but it, too, is concerned not
with doctrine, but with morality: "And when they are
chosen who are set apart to receive baptism let their life
be examined, whether they lived piously while catechumens . . . whether they visited the sick, whether they
have fulfilled every good work" (pp. 30–31). If they survive this scrutiny, the candidates are then allowed to
"hear the gospel" (p. 31), that is, to receive instruction in
the Scriptures and the Creed.[14] Nor does this end the period of scrutiny; for "when the day draws near on which
they are to be baptized, let the bishop exorcise each one
of them, that he may be certain that he is purified; but if
there is one who is not purified, let him be put on one side
because he did not hear the word of instruction with
faith" (p. 31). Even though the lectures heard by the candidates become gradually more theological, their basis in

13. Dix, *Treatise*, p. 23.
14. See also *Peregrinatio Etheriae*, p. 574.

moral precept and example (a basis that has its origins in the tradition of Jewish catechetics) is never forgotten; for it is on this foundation that the catechists build a structure of understanding, which, when it is complete, stands ready to be the receptacle of the deepest mysteries:

> It has long been my wish, true-born and long-desired children of the Church, to discourse to you upon these spiritual, heavenly mysteries. . . . I delayed until the present occasion, calculating that after what you saw on that night [of the Easter Vigil] I should find you a readier audience now when I am to be your guide to the brighter and more fragrant meadows of this second Eden. In particular, you are now capable of understanding the diviner mysteries of divine, life-giving baptism.[15]

As we have seen, progress toward this capability is marked on three distinct but correlated scales. The first is liturgical, and brings the catechumen from a position outside the community to Baptism, from Baptism to a place at the Lord's Supper, and from a first and second partaking of that Supper to full membership in the Church Militant. The second is stational, and brings the catechumen from a position outside the Church to its porch, from the porch to the baptistry, from the baptistry to the altar, and from a second approach to the altar to an exit from the Church which now is relocated within him. The third is educational, and it proceeds from an instruction in morality and self-discipline, to a hearing of the Creed and the Law, and finally to an immersion in those

15. *The Works of Saint Cyril,* vol. II, p. 153. See also *Peregrinatio Etheriae*, p. 575. It is now thought that the five Mystagogical or Easter lectures were written not by Cyril, but by his successor, John II, Bishop of Jerusalem, 387–417. In the edition available to the Reformation catechists (Cologne, 1564) the attribution to Cyril is not challenged.

deeper mysteries that will be apprehended only by those whose understandings have been raised and illuminated by the course of studies they have undergone. On all three scales the catechumen is brought to the Church—to its building, to its ceremonies, to the doctrine that finally constitutes it—and then exits from it; but he leaves only because everything the Church stands for (in two senses) has been interiorized. By joining the faithful he has *become* the goal to which his steps were leading him; for, "Know ye not that ye are the temple of God, and that the Spirit of God dwelleth in you?"

2. LET A MAN EXAMINE HIMSELF

This, then, was the extended catechumenate as it flourished in the fourth century and as it is remembered in the catechisms of the Reformation. It is also remembered by Herbert, who borrows its divisions to demarcate the sections of his sequence of poems and then entitles the sequence *The Temple*, thus linking it even more firmly to a tradition in which that word has so powerful and precise a range of associations. It is because of this range that it is at once impossible and unnecessary to specify the exact source of Herbert's invention. It is possible that he took his cue directly from Charcke who urges learning out of catechisms "as it were in the Porche of the temple" before "being let into the Sanctuary" and "the last and deepest mysteries," or from Stockwood who recalls that in the Primitive Church those who had not yet passed through the first stage of catechetical instruction were "suffered not . . . to come once within the Church, but kept . . . aloofe without, in a place by themselves, as it might bee now with us the Church Porche." He may well have read Becon or Bourne or Bastingius or Holland or J.F. or Crooke or T.W. or Jewel or E.B. or Hooker, all of whom give accounts of the catechumenate and its procedures. He certainly did read Augustine and quite probably Cyril and it is likely that he discussed them with Andrewes, who refers to their catechisms in his own. He could not have helped but know the commentaries in which catechists are characterized as temple-builders, and the prefaces in which the same characterization is made from the other direction. His interest in pedagogical techniques would have made him familiar with the appropriation by educational theorists of the Church Porch —Church—Sanctuary sequence, and he may have recalled the letter of Erasmus in which the course of study in Colet's school is described as beginning in the Porch where stood the "Catechumens, or the Children to be instructed in the principles of Religion; where no Child is to be admitted, but what can read or write."[16] He may well have been struck by the frontispiece to John Mayer's *The English Catechisme Or A Commentarie On the Short Catechisme set forth in the Booke of Common Prayer. Wherin All necessarie Questions touching the Christian Faith are inserted, scandals removed, moderne Controversies handled, doubts resolved, and many Cases of Conscience cleared. Profitable for Ministers in their Churches, for Schoole-masters in their Schooles, and for Householders in their Families.* Facing this title page is a picture of a temple. Three steps labelled Faith, Hope, and Charitie lead up to it. The building itself

16. Quoted by S. J. Curtis in *History of Education in Great Britain* (London, 1965), p. 77. See also John Brinsley, *Ludus literarius; or the grammar schools* (1627), in the edition of E. T. Campagnac (Liverpool and London, 1917), p. 147; and William Coles, *The art of simpling* (1657), p. 13: "So much for the Porch. We come now to the structure."

יהוה

My house shal be called the house of prayer

Lord heare, of prayers, and let our cryes come unto thee

THE English CATECHISME by IOHN MAYER B.ʳ of Diuinity. Printed for IOHN MARRIOTT 1621.

CHARITIE
HOPE
FAITH

Christ the

Rock

The place for malefactors and such as fall from the Church.

THE
ENGLISH
Catechisme.

OR
A COMMENTA-
RIE ON THE SHORT
CATECHISME set forth in the
Booke of Common Prayer.

Rirk.   Lut.

WHEREIN,
All necessarie Questions touching
the Christian Faith are inserted, scandals remo-
ued, moderne Controuersies handled, doubts
resolued, and many Cases of Conscience
cleared.

Profitable for Ministers in their Churches, for Schoole-
masters in their Schooles, and for Housholders
in their Families.

By IOHN MAYER Bachelour of
Diuinitie.

LONDON,
Printed for IOHN MARRIOT, and are to be sold
at his Shop in Saint Dunstans Churchyard in
Fleetstreet. 1621.

is divided into three parts: a large central section, obviously the Church proper, is flanked by two semi-enclosed porches. In one, children are being catechized by an instructor who calls in the words of the Psalmist: "Come unto me ye Children and I will teach you the feare of the Lord." (We should recall that David was considered the type of the catechist and is the figure to whom Herbert is most often compared.) In the other, a group of older worshippers cries, "Lord, hear our prayers and let our cryes come unto thee." This tableau is centered on the page. Above and below it are details that qualify the apparent independence of the actors. Everyone in the scene is looking upward and is being looked down upon by two eyes; these eyes are placed at the border of the sun in the center of which is written YHWH, the Hebrew acronym for God. The beams of light that extend from the two eyes terminate in cartoon-like scrolls which contain the words of the catechist on one side and of the praying elders on the other. As a result, it is impossible to tell whether these words proceed from their putative speakers or from the God to whom they are directed. Underneath the Temple, a cutaway reveals that it is supported not by the man-made pillars, but by a pillar-like formation of rocks across which is written *Christ the Rock*. This is obviously a pictorial realization of the topos of the foundations:[17] on this rock, and no other, does the Temple stand, and it is the foundation and true cause of all that is done within the Temple, including the making of those living temples

17. It could well be an illustration of Andrewes's words: The foundation "must be digged deepe, till we come to the Rocke" (*A patterne,* pp. 13–14). See also William Whitaker, *A shorte summe of christianity delivered by way of catechisme* (1630), sig. A4ᵛ: "If they build on this Rocky Foundation . . . the gates of Hell . . . shall not prevaile against them."

whose edification is the catechist's goal. The central panel is very much like the engraving that illustrates "Superliminare" in the 1674 edition of *The Temple*. But in the engraving the door to the Church is open and through it one sees the parishioners and the parson. In Mayer's frontispiece, on the other hand, the door is closed because it serves as a surface for the inscription of the title, *The English Catechism by John Mayer B^r. of Divinity*. The meaning is clear: only when the course of study to be negotiated in this book is completed will its readers be allowed to enter the Church proper; until then they remain, along with those depicted in the frontispiece, on the church porch.

If Herbert did see this frontispiece, he would also have read the introductory prayer to the edition of 1623 in which Mayer asks that he, along with his readers, be made by the Master-builder a living stone "upon the right foundation . . . till that all the building couple together, groweth into an holy Temple in the Lord." In any case, it is no more necessary to verify this speculation than it is to choose between the possibilities rehearsed in the preceding paragraph. When so many paths are available, proof that one was taken is almost beside the point. Indeed it would have been remarkable had Herbert *not* hit upon the sequence of the catechumenate as an organizational scheme, given its prominence in homiletic literature, his own interest in catechizing and in the effect of his poetry on its readers, and his statement in *The Country Parson* that catechisms are the foundation of a course of knowledge that ends in the building of "a spirituall Temple." As it is, the correspondence between the stages of the catechumenate and the divisions of *The Temple* is sufficiently striking to constitute an argument by itself, without the support of additional evidence: the instructional sequence is the same, from relatively easy rules of morality and civility ("The Church-porch") to the deeper mysteries of the creed and the sacraments (in "The Church") to the history of salvation ("The Church Militant"); the sequence of movement is the same, from the church porch to the baptistry, from the baptistry to the altar, and from the altar out into the ranks of the faithful; and the liturgical sequence is roughly the same, from prebaptismal instruction (in "The Church-porch"), to baptism itself (in or just before "Superliminare"), to a first communion ("The Altar") followed, after a period of advanced instruction, by a second communion ("Love III") and concluding in the joining of the Church Militant ("The Church Militant").

This last set of equivalences is less than exact because the youth to whom *The Temple* is addressed has already been baptized, and therefore his progress cannot be said to parallel that of the catechumen. The two careers can be seen as aligned, however, if we remember that in the liturgy of the *Book of Common Prayer*, confirmation completes what was begun in baptism by requiring a reaffirmation of the profession of faith made for the infant by his godparents:

When children come to the years of discretion and have learned what their godfathers and godmothers promised for them in Baptism, they may then themselves with their own mouth, and with their own consent, openly before the church ratify and confirm the same.[18]

It is this rubric that supports Brewster Ford's character-

18. *The Book of Common Prayer, 1559*, ed. J. E. Booty (Charlottesville, Va., 1976), p. 282.

ization of the "Church-porch" as an "initiatory poem" which is "sacramentally analogous to baptism."[19] The analogy, as John David Walker points out,[20] is metaphoric rather than literal, and because it is metaphoric, the "Church-porch"–"Superliminare" sequence is able to function simultaneously in two liturgical patterns; at once recalling the course of the early catechumenate (in which the instruction on the porch *is* prebaptismal), and acknowledging the changes that have come about as a result of the shift from infant to adult baptism.

The change that most concerns us here is in the relationship of the catechism to the sacraments. Catechizing, as William Basset observes, "is in order to Baptism in the Children of Infidels . . . but it is in order to Confirmation, and the Sacrament of the Supper in the Children of Christians, who are baptiz'd already."[21] That is, while in the early church catechizing is preliminary to baptism, for Herbert and his readers it is part of the preparation to receive communion: "There shall none be admitted to the Holy Communion, until such time as he can say the catechism, and be confirmed."[22] This link between catechizing and communion is reflected in the full title of catechisms like Frewen's:

Certaine choise grounds and principles of our Christian religion . . . Wherin the people of the Parish of Northiham . . . have been Catechized, and instructed, for the settling of their hearts and mindes,

19. *The Influence of the Prayer Book Calendar on the Shape of George Herbert's The Temple.* Diss. University of Virginia, 1964, p. 106.
20. "Architectonics," p. 293.
21. *A discourse on my lord-archbishop's of Canterbury's . . . letters* (1684), pp. 7–8.
22. *Book of Common Prayer,* p. 289.

in the mysteries of salvation, and for their better preparation to the Lords Supper. [23]

The pressure for "better preparation" is exerted by the dire warnings of I Corinthians 11:27, 29:

Wherefore whosoever shall eat this bread, and drink this cup of the Lord, unworthily, shall be guilty of the body and blood of the Lord. . . . For he that eateth and drinketh unworthily, eateth and drinketh damnation to himself.

These dreadful warnings are repeated in the Prayer Book, and they are often cited by those who enumerate the benefits of learning the catechism. "The Holy Ghost plainely affirmeth of the other sort [those who are not prepared] that they eate and drinke their own judgement." "Can it be denied," asks E. B. "that this is one special good helpe of preparation to be well lessoned in all the ground points of the Christian doctrine?"[24] In *The common catechisme* of Richard Bernard (1630), the Questioner asks "Why is it [the catechism] to be learned before any come to the Sacrament," and the predictable answer comes back: "Because by the knowledge therof they may be better prepared thereunto, without which preparation they are not counted fit to be communicants" (sig. A5^r).

While catechizing is a "good helpe of preparation," it is

23. See also H. Graie, *A short and easie introduction to christian faith. Conteining the summe of the principles of Religion, necessary to be knowne of all before they presume to receive the Sacrament of the Lords Supper* (1588); *A catechisme in briefe questions and answeres. Containing such Things as are to be knowne or had by all such as would partake the Sacrament of the Lord's Supper with Comfort* (Oxford, 1629); Edward Fenton, *So shorte a catechisme, that whosoever cannot, or wil not learne, are not in any wise to be admitted to the Lords Supper* (1626); Marten Micron, *A short and faythful instruction for symple christianes whych intende worthely to receyve the holy supper* (1560).

24. *A Catechisme or Briefe Instruction*, sig. A3^v.

by no means all-sufficient and it is itself preliminary to the performance of another duty which Paul enjoins in I Corinthians 11:28: "But let a man examine himself, and so let him eat of that bread, and drink of that cup." Self-examination is necessary, the catechists tell us, because while another can test one's ability to recite the creed or rehearse doctrine, *"none* can try or examine *thee,* so well as thou canst try *thy selfe.* For *thou* knowest more by thy selfe then *all* the world beside doth. Thou knowest *certainly* whether thou dost *truly repent* and *beleeve* stedfastly in *Christ* thy Saviour, which none but God and thine owne soule can certainly affirme."[25] This does not mean

that the *Church of England* doth . . . barre the *Minister* from examining *his flocke* whether they bee furnished with *competent knowledge* concerning the *nature* and *use* of the Sacrament: but yet *it* holdeth it not *sufficient* that a communicant have his *Pastors approbation* and allowance; but *it* requires also, that wee *our selves* should enter into our *own hearts,* and call our *owne conscience* to examination. (p. 26)

The catechists are aware that some will be tempted to discharge one obligation by slighting the other. Bourne confronts the problem directly by having his questioner raise it: *"But doth not the holy Apostle* Paul *require a man to examine himself? What then need any man or woman, or childe, give an Answer to the Examination or Question of another?"*[26] The answer defines the relationship between the duties; the "competent measure" of knowledge acquired by learning the catechism is itself "requisite to

25. Theophilus Field, *Parasceve Paschae: or a Christians preparation to the worthy receiving of the blessed Sacrament of the Lords supper* (1624), pp. 25–26.
26. *A light,* p. 2.

enable [men] to examine themselves (as the Scripture, and the spirit of Christ in the Scriptures require)'' (p. 4). The two examinations are not separate activities, but stages in a single effort of preparation, and, as the instructions of Thomas Cartwright indicate, the stages are ordered:

Q. *How are we to prepare ourselves . . . ?*
A. Wee are, first, to examine our knowledge, as in the grounds and principles of religion; . . . Secondly, wee are to examine what faith wee have and what repentance; not onely in the generall but for our particular sinnes; whether we doe bewaile them, or judge ourselves for them.[27]

Obviously, the first step could not be taken if the communicant had not undergone catechistical instruction; he is, in effect, asked to give himself a review course and to play the Bishop's role as well as his own. This done, he can turn to the more difficult and rigorous task of taking personal inventory. This will not be a movement away from catechizing, but a passing to a catechism of a different kind, a private catechism, which, while its questions are not formal and set, is nevertheless codified. The formula varies, but within a limited range; and Alexander Nowell's formulation is full and representative:

M.   What is our dutie to doe, that we may come rightly to the Lords Supper?
Sch.   To examine ourselves whether we be true members of Christ.
M.   By what tokens shall we know this?

27. *A treatise of Christian religion, Or The Whole Bodie and Substance of Divinitie* (1616), p. 232. See also Bernard, *The common catechisme,* sig. A4[r], where the reader is told that one of the reasons catechisms are learned is because they make us "able to examine ourselves of our faith, of our duties to God and man."

Sch. First if we heartily repent us of our sinne; next, if we stay our selves and rest in a sure hope of Gods mercies through Christ, with a thankefull remembrance of our redemption purchased by his death. Moreover, if we conceive an earnest minde & determinate purpose to lead our life godly hereafter. Finally seeing in the Lords Supper is conteined a token of friendship & love among men, if we have brotherly love to our neighbor; that is to all men, without any evill or hatred.[28]

The second of Nowell's "tokens" is answerable to another of the biblical injunctions directed at the would-be communicant: "this do ye . . . in remembrance of me" (I Corinthians 11:25). In some catechisms, this aspect of preparation is stressed more than any other. It is necessary, declares Henry Vesey, "that we lift up thankfull hearts unto our Lord God for the great mercie of our Redemption."[29] This thankfulness, declares Thomas Ratcliffe, is "the first thing that you must bring with you when you come to be partaken of the Sacrament," and it is to be offered "to God onely."[30] What this means is that you are not to attribute the grace you are about to receive to your own merits. To come worthily to the Lord's Supper is not to *be* worthy, but to know that you are not. I am a "worthie receiver," declares Arthur Dent, "if I examine my selfe and find that I humbly ac-

28. *A catechisme or institution of christian religion* (1614), sig. M3ᵛ. For similar formulations see Thomas Vicars, *The grounds of that doctrine which is according to godlinesse or a briefe and easie catechisme (gathered out of many other, Dr. Cranmer, Dr. Nowell, Mr. Perkins, Mr. Paget, Mr. Egerton, Mr. Fenton, Mr. Bristow)*, 3rd edition (1631), p. 18; Stephen Denison, *A compendious catechisme* (1621), p. 10; Samuel Browne, *The summe of Christian religion* (1630), sigs. C4ᵛ-C5ʳ.

29. *The scope of the scripture* (1621), p. 48.

30. *A short summe of the whole catechisme* (1619), sig. C2ᵛ.

knowledge mine own unworthiness." With no basis of
hope in his own actions, he can then turn to the actions of
another, "assuredly resting upon promises of pardon
made in Christ." "Then," he concludes, "am I worthy,
because mine unworthiness is forgiven, and put out of
remembrance."[31] In the logic of redemption, worthiness
proceeds from a conviction of unworthiness, one's sins
are forgotten because one remembers, and in the end a
proper balance between contrition and faithful hope
brings one to the Lord's Supper prepared.

That balance can be upset, however, by the very success of the self-examination designed to achieve it; for
knowledge of our sins and of our inability to avoid com-
mitting them can become a burden so great that we conclude ourselves undeserving and fear to come to the holy
table lest we eat and drink damnation and be guilty of the
body and blood of the Lord. It is "this feare," Daniel
Rogers reminds us, "the end of the sacrament is to rid
thee of." Remember that, "lest thou shouldst stagger
about thy right and part herin."[32] Yet it is almost inevitable that he who examines himself will stagger, for "suche
a scrupulous ripping up of all and every his sinnes, with
all their circumstances, cannot but *anguish* and torment
the soule with *doubts, diffidence* and *despaire.*"[33] "Not-
withstanding," Yves Rouspeau advises, "so farre it is
that the imperfections which are in us should cause us to
drawe back . . . from this holy banquet, that rather . . .
they oughte to cause us to come the sooner, to the in-
tent that as poore famished creatures, we might more

31. *A pastime for parents* (1606), sig. G6ʳ.
32. *A practicall catechisme* (1632), p. 82.
33. *Parasceve Paschae*, p. 24.

greedily and with greater desire, receive Jesus Christ."[34]
William Perkins carries this argument to its logical conclusion: "If being thus prepared, thou feelst that thou has
a corrupt & rebellious heart, know this: that thou are then
well disposed to the Lords Table." Ideally, men should
"bring pure and sound hearts" to the Lord's Supper, but
since that sacrament is principally a "medicine to the
diseased and languishing soule," it is entirely fitting that
men "seeke to purifie and heale their hearts in it."[35] Vicars cites Psalm 5 to make the same point: "The *sacrifice of
God is a broken Spirit*, a *broken* and a contrite heart, O God,
thou will not despise."[36] Not only is a broken and bruised
heart acceptable, it is required: "That broken heart thou
wouldst faine have in the searching and lamenting of thy
sinnes, nourish daily; he that in a great frost would keepe
the yce thin, must keepe it broken everyday: so thou, thy
soule-issues, lest thine heart harden."[37]

As the catechists urge these arguments, they place
their charges on the horns of a dilemma: if the medicine
of the sacrament is to be efficacious, the soul must feel its
need of it, "This heavenly feast is a medicine for all them
that be sicke in soul"; but the soul that feels its sickness
too strongly will be "terrified, and discouraged from the
partaking of this Sacrament."[38] If one decides to stay
away, in order to avoid eating and drinking damnation,
he only incurs what he would avoid. "Thus we see," cries

34. *A treatise of the preparation to the holy supper* (1579), sig. D4ᵛ.

35. *The foundation of Christian religion* (1612), p. 76.

36. *The grounds*, p. 19.

37. Rogers, *A practicall catechisme*, p. 82. For a discussion of the doctrine of preparation see Norman Petitt, *The Heart Prepared: Grace and
Conversion in Puritan Spiritual Life* (New Haven, 1966).

38. John Frewen, *Certaine choise grounds*, pp. 373, 371.

John Mayer," what a maze or labyrinth sin doth bring
men into; in danger they are by comming, and in danger
by not comming to the Lords Table."[39] Literally, he is
damned if he does, and damned if he does not: *"He may
not keepe away from the Lords Supper, for this were a provoking
of God to wrath: neither can hee come unto it, without offending
the Lord in a higher degree"* (p. 573).

"What," asks Mayer, "may a man doe then in this
case?" (p. 574). The answer is, he may do nothing—that
is the point of the impasse at which he finds himself—but
he may turn to another: *"He must humbly sue unto God for
the pardon of all his sins, to strike his hard heart, that he may
melt into teares for them"* (p. 573). The Lord, Frewen assures us, "will not faile to be gracious and mercifull for
Christs sake. For hee knoweth our corruptions and imperfections, and will have regard of our infirmities" (p.
372). "Hee that breaketh not a bruised rede will not cast
us off because of our infirmities" (p. 374). These answers
do not so much resolve the dilemma as rise above it to the
all-resolving logic of love:

And if I aske the reason, why *God* gave his *Sonne* to doe and
suffer *all this* for my sake, or why the *Sonne* of God would suffer
it? I shall find *none,* but the great and *infinite love* to *me,* who
deserved no love at all. . . . It was in God, his incomprehen-
sible love. . . . *This love* of Gods is a *Sic* without any Sicut;
beyond all comparison; nothing that ever was, or shall bee,
may stand in comparison with it."[40]

Or, in other words, do ye this in remembrance of me.

It might seem that we have wandered from our primary concern, but these texts are intimately related to in-

39. *The English catechisme* (1621), p. 574.
40. *Parasceve Paschae,* p. 244.

dividual poems and groups of poems in "The Church": "Faith" follows "Repentance" just as it does in the order of self-examination, and only "Prayer I" separates them from "The H. Communion." Later the sequence is repeated: In "The Invitation" sinners are bid "Come ye hither . . . Bringing all your sinnes"; "Taste and fear not," they are told, for "Here is love" (lines 13, 15, 16, 28). The next poem is "The Banquet" and in it the bruised and broken heart of the communicant is mended by the remembrance of Christ's bruised and broken body:

> . . . As Pomanders and wood
> > Still are good,
> Yet being bruis'd are better sented:
> God, to show how farre his love
> > Could improve,
> Here, as broken, is presented.
> > (lines 25-30)

The heart, however, cannot take what is presented, even when it is offered by Love:

> Love bade me welcome: yet my soul drew back,
> > Guiltie of dust and sinne.
> > > ("Love III")

Still doubting his worthiness ("A guest, I answer'd, worthy to be here"), and burdened by sin ("I the unkinde, ungratefull?"), the communicant must once again be reminded of what he is to remember ("And know you not, sayes Love, who bore the blame?") before he is finally prepared (in two senses) to partake: "So I did sit and eat." This poem concludes "The Church" but it also returns us to its beginning, to "The Altar" where a broken heart finds the offering of a broken body, to "The Sacrifice" and the act in relation to which the heart must prepare itself, to "The Thanksgiving" where the communicant finds that preparing himself is a task more difficult than he had imagined, and finally to "The Reprisall" where the difficulty is overcome by admitting that *he* cannot overcome it:

Though I can do nought/ Against thee, in thee I will overcome.
(lines 15–16)

It is clear that we are dealing here not with a single linear pattern, but with a *rhythm*, and it is a rhythm whose fluctuations are bounded by the two poles between which self-examination moves, repentance and faith. Attached to these poles are two corollary dangers: on the one hand, the obligation of "every man in his own heart and *estimation*" to "set himself *low*, and become *vile* in his own eyes"[41] can lead to despair and a sense of hopelessness; and on the other, the man who rests "in a sure hope of Gods mercies"[42] may rest there too complacently, and lose the benefit of his faith by being proud of it; for "Whosoever then stand upon their owne Righteousness, and thinke to be saved by the least measure, part, or contribution of their owne workes or merits, have no part in the New Testament, and so have nothing to doe with this Sacrament."[43] The first danger is courted in poems like "Sinne" (I and II), "Sepulchre," "Dialogue," "Grief," "Sinnes round," "The Method," "Unkindnesse," "Ungratefulness," and of course "Love III"; the second is explored in "The Thanksgiving," "The Reprisall," "The Holdfast," "The Pearl," "The Crosse,"

41. *Ibid.*, pp. 168–169.
42. Nowell, *A catechisme* (1614), sig. M3ᵛ.
43. John Randall, *Three and twentie sermons, or, catechisticall lectures upon the Sacrament of the Lords Supper* (1638), p. 199.

"Miserie," "Love I," "Love II," "Jordan I," and "Jordan II." These poems do not form a pattern, but enter into patterned relationships with their neighbors. In "Businesse" the complaint (uttered in the form of catechistical questions: "Who di'd for thee?") is that the soul does not feel sin strongly enough:

> Canst be idle? canst thou play,
> Foolish soul who sinn'd to day?
> (lines 1–2)

It is "sighs and grones" (line 12) that are required because

> Who in heart not ever kneels,
> Neither sinne nor Saviour feels
> (lines 37–38)

In "Dialogue," the very next poem, the soul feels sin too strongly, and declares itself not "worth the having" because it is "so full of stains" (lines 3, 7). Both poems are responses to the call in "The Dawning"—"Awake sad heart . . . And with a thankfull heart his comforts take" (lines 1, 6)—which in turn follows directly upon the urgings of "Vanitie" (II):

> O heare betimes, lest thy relenting
> May come too late!
> To Purchase heaven for repenting
> Is no hard rate.
>   (lines 7-10)

The rate may not be hard, but when it is paid, in "Dialogue," there is nothing left over for which or with which to be thankful: "What delight or hope remains?" (line 8). Caught on the horns of the worthiness-unworthiness dilemma, the speaker can only complain:

> But as I can see no merit,
> Leading to this favour:

> So the way to fit me for it
> Is beyond my savour.
> (lines 17-20)

Precisely. He can see no merit, because the merit is not his; the way to fitness has been marked out by another, and it is that other who asks his creature to:

> *Follow my resigning:*
> *That as I did freely part*
> *With my glorie and desert,*
> *Left all joyes to feel all smart.*
> (lines 28-31)

Or, in other words, do ye this in remembrance of *me*, a remembrance that, because it is too much for the speaker, brings about the state he was unable to achieve: "Ah! no more: thou break'st my heart" (line 32). A heart broken is a heart prepared. Self-examination has apparently done its work, moving, in the prescribed manner, from conviction of sin to repentance, and from repentance to a thankful remembrance of mercy. Any yet in the next poem, "Dulnesse," the heart is hard again, the spirit is once more "lost in flesh" (line 21), and the sequence begins anew, with poems like "Hope," "Sinnes round," "Gratefulnesse," "Confession," and "Giddinesse," leading to the inevitable sacramental lyric, "The Bunch of Grapes."[44]

It follows that the attempt to find a significance in the arrangement of the poems is misconceived, at least insofar as it has as its goal a single and consecutive pattern

44. See the detailed analysis of this poem in my "Catechizing the Reader: Herbert's Socratean Rhetoric," in *The Rhetoric of Renaissance Poetry*, ed. T. Sloan and R. Waddington (Berkeley and Los Angeles, 1974), pp. 179–185.

(a tour of an English Church, the progress of the liturgical year) that works itself out in the space between "The Altar" and "Love III." It is sometimes assumed that the choice is between discovering such a pattern or concluding that the order is random, either because Herbert had no plan, or because the plan he had in mind was left unexecuted. But if for a plan we substitute a project, the project of preparing oneself worthily to receive the sacrament,[45] then it is possible to assert that the order is random *and* patterned. It is patterned because the points of self-examination are finite—repentance, faith, charity, the amendment of life; and it is random because each point harbors its special danger into which the self-examiner may be falling even as he thinks to satisfy it. As a result, there is no straightforward path to success in this exercise (indeed the assumption of such a path is the surest way to miss it); instead there is only a succession of approaches and the possibility at every step of embracing the very error one seeks to avoid.

In short, while the content of self-examination is stable, its course is unpredictable. (Here, then, is another source for the "uniquely Herbertian quality of order and surprise.")[46] What is predictable is that "the plateau of assurance" to which Martz believes the sequence rises is never achieved; or, if it seems for a moment to be achieved, the achievement is never sustained. ("To have my aim, and yet to be/ Further from it then when I bent

45. It is a nice coincidence that "one poem by Herbert appears as a hymn in *Sacramental Hymns collected (chiefly) out of such passages of the New Testament as contain the most suitable matter of Divine Praises in the celebration of the Lord's Supper* (1693)." Reported in Ray, p. 262.

46. Coburn Freer, *Music for a King*, p. 218.

my bow.''[47]) To the original injunction, "let a man examine himself," we must add a coda: "let a man examine himself again and again and again." No point is made more often in the catechisms than the necessity of coming often to the Lord's Supper. "Baptisme is but once administered," declares I. G., "but the Lords Supper is often to be received."[48] As with any other nourishment, explains Nowell, "we need oft to fede."[49] "Let us not abstain," warns Cranmer, "let us . . . go to this godly supper."[50] It follows that every approach to the altar will be a new occasion for self-examination: *"By the oft and worthy partaking therof, we are . . . provoked to a more serious examination of our spirituall estate."*[51] Examine, approach, examine; the rhythm is iterative and endless, as one duty gives way necessarily to the other: "Be quickened to examine your selves, and search your Hearts and lives, and practise your repentance, and stirre up your Faith . . . and to put forth your best endevors for your sitting to that heavenly worke. After the Sacrament is received, the same points to be rehearsed againe. . . . ''[52]

It is a rhythm that precludes closure and yet closure is what it invites by repeatedly holding out, and then defaulting on, the promise of stability and rest. The speakers of Herbert's poems often complain that a state of equilibrium can never be maintained: "Joy, I did lock thee

47. "The Crosse," lines 25–26.

48. *The Christians profession* (1630), p. 69.

49. *A catechisme* (1593), sig. f6^v.

50. Thomas Cranmer, *Catechismus: That is to say; a shorte instruction into Christian religion* (1548), sig. Jjv^r.

51. Nicholas Byfield, *The principall grounds of Christian religion* (1625), p. 19.

52. John Randall, *Three and twentie sermons*, pp. 3–4.

up: but some bad man/hath let thee out again" ("The Bunch of Grapes," lines 1–2); "At first thou gav'st me milk and sweetnesses;/I had my wish and way" ("Affliction I," lines 19–20); "Although there were some fourtie heav'ns, or more,/Sometimes I peere above them all;/ Sometimes I hardly reach a score,/Sometimes to hell I fall" ("The Temper I," lines 5–8). Even the inverted equanimity of a long sojourn in hell is not allowed: "Who would have thought my shrivel'd heart / Could have re-cover'd greennesse?" ("The Flower," lines 8–9). The re-covery, while it is welcome, is also disquieting, because it deprives the speaker of the security that any regularized pattern, even a negative one, can provide. As readers and critics we are similarly deprived of pattern and simi-larly tempted by its intermittent availability, as we too enjoy apparent (interpretive) successes and achieve sup-posedly full understandings, only to find again and again that the successes are temporary and the understandings partial. If the never-ending process of self-examination is what these poems record, it is also what they provoke.

Herbert tells us as much when he invites us to ap-proach the altar:

Superliminare

Thou, whom the former precepts have
Sprinkled and taught, how to behave
Thy self in church; approach, and taste
The churches mysticall repast.

Avoid Profanenesse; come not here:
Nothing but holy, pure, and cleare,
Or that which groneth to be so,
May at his perill further go.

This is a very important poem in the larger structure of

The Temple because it both confirms and refines the catechistical context in which the poems are to be read. The confirmation is the work of the first stanza. Herbert begins by re-addressing the "youth" whom the opening lines of "The Church-porch" mark "for a treasure." This is not, I think, the "worldly young man" of Summers's argument,[53] but a more general designation for the youths to whom catechisms were customarily addressed.[54] To be sure, many were dedicated to children of the nobility (or in Cranmer's case to a young monarch), but the scope of the intended audience is more fairly represented by titles like *An Helpe For Yong people Preparing them for the worthy receiving of the Lords Supper* (by W. L.) or *Joshuas godly resolution with Caleb, . . . A twofold Catechisme for instruction of youth* (by Richard Bernard, 1612).[55]

It is these youths who were said to be "sprinkled" with "precepts," a reference to the prominence in the catechism of the Decalogue. In the Vulgate (Exodus 20:6) and in the Latin catechisms of Calvin, Nowell, and Poynet, the word for commandments is *praecepta*, and in the period from the late Middle Ages through the seventeenth cen-

53. *George Herbert,* pp. 103–104.

54. On this and other points see the unpublished dissertation of Brewster Ford, *The Influence of the Prayer Book,* pp. 24–37. Once again corroborating evidence of a kind is available in the seventeenth century response to Herbert's poetry which was used, we are told, by one who turned the poems into hymns "to teach Children to Spell." Reported in Ray, p. 269.

55. E. B.'s catechism is addressed to "Christian Parents, Householders, Schoole-masters, and such as have charge of youth" (sig. A3^r). Frewen's *Certaine choise grounds* is dedicated "To The Young And Worthy Knight, Sir John Hare . . . And to the vertuous yong Lady, the Lady Elizabeth . . . and to her brother, the hopefull yong Gentleman."

tury, the Ten Commandments are often referred to as the Ten Precepts.[56] (Several instances are cited in the *OED* under "precept.") To be catechized, then, is to be instructed in (or sprinkled with) "the precepts," and Thomas Comber recalls that it was the Jewish practice to bring children to the Temple, where, after having been "publickly examined," they were then "declared to be Children of the Precept."[57] It was "up to this catechizing," he adds, that "our Saviour came," and it is in this context that Nowell urges a return to the primitive practice of examining children "whether they were skilled in the precepts of religion or no."[58] Samuel Crooke observes that by catechizing is signified "such a kind of teaching, as doth by little and little (*line unto line, precept unto precept* . . .) inform."[59] Crooke cites as his source Isaiah 28:13 ("the word of the Lord was unto them precept upon precept"), a favorite text of the catechists which is also appropriated by Arthur Dent: "We must . . . tell them one thing, twentie times . . . here a little and there a little, precept upon precept, as the prophet speaketh."[60] "There will alwayes be," says T. W., "such rude and ignorant ones as will need the principles, and must have precept upon precept."[61]

56. See also Augustine, *De Catechizandis Rudibus*, ed. G. Krüger (Tübingen, 1934), p. 12: "*Simul etiam praecepta breviter et decenter commemorentur Christianae atque honestae conversationis.*" Reverend Christopher, in his edition of this tract (Westminster, Md., 1946), declares that "there is no doubt that when Augustine uses the term [precepts], he is referring to the Decalogue" (p. 95).

57. *A companion to the temple* (1679), p. 615.

58. *A catechisme*, ed. G. E. Corrie, p. 211.

59. *The guide unto true blessednesse*, sig. B2^r.

60. *The plaine mans path-way to Heaven* (1603), p. 332.

61. *An exposition*, p. 5.

"Precepts" is thus a particularly appropriate word to designate "The Church-porch," a poem of "prudential advice"[62] that has been called "pre-Christian"[63] because it is concerned with the moral and outward part of the Law.[64] Its tone and scope correspond to the lists of rules that were often appended to Reformation catechisms. These rules are limited for the most part to the norms of social and civil decorums—"Marke the life and be-haviour of the wicked,"[65] "I must take heed what company I keepe,"[66] "that . . . the time be redeemed which hath been idely, carelessly, unprofitably spent"[67]—and one may conform to them without ever confronting the problem of living a life that conforms to the teachings of Christ. This limitation is reflected in the carefully circum-scribed claim made for "The Church-porch" in "Super-luminare": to have read it is to know "how to behave / Thy self in church." That is, you will know how to re-move your hat ("Be bare," line 403), to pay attention ("Let vain or busie thoughts have there no part," line 421), and to be respectful of the parson ("Jest not at preachers language, or expression," line 439).

In other words, this first stanza of "Superluminare" identifies "The Church-porch" as a catechistical poem and extends an invitation ("approach and taste") to those

62. Freer, *Music For a King,* p. 145.

63. Joseph Summers, introduction to *The Selected Poems of George Her-bert* (New York, 1967), p. xxii.

64. See Halewood, *The Poetry of Grace,* p. 96, and Brewster Ford, *The Influence of the Prayer Book,* p. 24.

65. Stephen Egerton, *A briefe methode of catechizing,* 16th ed. (1608), p. 47. The section is headed "Certaine Rules for the direction of a Christian life."

66. Richard Bernard, *A double catechisme* (Cambridge, 1657), p. 41.

67. Edmund Coote, *The English Scholemaister* (1614), p. 39. The sec-tion is headed, *"Sundry necessary observations for a Christian."*

who by reading it have become children of the precept.[68]
In the second stanza, however, that invitation is qualified
and complicated. The complications begin with line 5:
"Avoid Profanenesse; come not here." Hutchinson, following Grosart and Palmer, places a comma after "Avoid"
because he wishes "to asist the modern reader" (p. 484).
What he fears is that this reader will take the phrase as a
straightforward exhortation rather than as a construction
in which Profaneness, personified, is ordered to with-
draw. Although this intransitive sense of "avoid" is certainly a possible one in 1633, the more modern sense is
equally available, and in the context a reader would be
likely to reach for it. He has, after all, just finished a 462-
line poem in which the sequence transitive-imperative-
object appears again and again. What could be more
natural than to assume that a final and summarizing injunction is intended here? That assumption, however,
will not survive the second half of the line ("come not
here"), for presumably it is precisely those who avoid
profaneness who should be bid to come. It is at this point
that a reader will revise his understanding of the syntax
in the direction of Hutchinson's emendation, and in so
doing, he will also revise his relationship to profaneness.
At first that relationship is one of agent to an abstraction
that is independent of him; but in the revised reading the
abstraction and the agent must be seen as inseparable;
profaneness cannot be avoided by moving away from it;
it resides within, and the line now asks to be read as an
accusation: Away, you profane person. Once again, in
the very process of adjusting to Herbert's verse we enact

68. On this point see George Ryley in Heissler, *Mr. Herbert's Temple,*
p. 38.

its meanings, moving from an external rule ("Avoid Profanenesse") to an interdiction that can only be escaped
by changing the self ("Avoid, Profanenesse").

In line 6 ("Nothing but holy, pure, and cleare"), both
the syntax and our position in the poem seem to stabilize,
and this is itself a comfort even though the statement it
seems to be making is hard and unyielding: only that
which is holy, pure, and clear can come. That statement
is apparently softened by the following line: "Or that
which groneth to be so." The qualifications for entry have
been relaxed by an exception that Arnold Stein is moved
to call "generous."[69] That generosity is withdrawn,
however, when in the last line the gate that had seemed
to open wide is suddenly straitened:

> May at his perill further go.

Without the phrase "at his perill," the line would confirm
our understanding of the quatrain as an effort to distinguish between those who can proceed safely and those
who cannot. That is, the resolved sense would be, only
those who are pure or wish to be so can further go. As
Herbert wrote it, however, the line denies safe passage to
everyone, because "at his perill" refers indifferently to all
the classes that have previously been established. Those
who are pure, those who would be so, those who are
not—all proceed at their peril. The scope of the modifier
is simply too large; it does not respect the distinctions we
have been encouraged to make, and in effect undoes
them.[70]

---

69. *George Herbert's Lyrics,* p. 13.
70. It is as if above the door of a public place were written the words:
"Only those who behave themselves or who are worrying about behav-
ing themselves are likely to encounter trouble."

It also undoes the confidence with which we as readers can proceed into "The Church." "Superliminare" is the perfect introduction to that section of *The Temple* because it resists reduction to a formula. It proposes conditions and then tells us that they cannot be met, or that if we meet them we are no less subject to the hazards of journeying. It issues an invitation we cannot refuse ("approach, and taste") and warns us of the consequences of accepting it. In short it marks our passage from one kind of catechizing, in which one hears and gives back clear and portable precepts, to another kind of catechizing, in which precepts are of no avail because a right answer or gesture is likely to be as perilous as a wrong one. In what follows we do approach and taste, not once but many times, and before and after each approach, we return to the task enjoined by the catechists and by the apostle: "Examine your selves, and search your Hearts and lives, and practise your repentance. . . . After the Sacrament is received, the same points to be rehearsed againe."

3. YOU MUST SIT DOWN AND EAT

Along with Herbert, we are still rehearsing them when "The Church" ends. In many ways "Love III" is a reprise of "Superluminare." Once again the communicant responds to an invitation ("Love bade me welcome") and makes, for the thousandth time, his "first entrance in." That entrance, even as it is hazarded, is forsworn ("my soul drew back") because the very reason for his need ("Guiltie of dust and sinne") is also the reason for his reluctance to have it supplied ("let my shame/ Go where it doth deserve"). He has taken seriously the injunction to "set himself low" and his success in self-examination has left him near despair: "I the unkinde, ungratefull? Ah my deare,/ I cannot look on thee." The all too familiar impasse has recurred: he must approach and taste if his soul is to receive its proper food; but if he approaches in a state of sin he will eat and drink damnation.

The resolution of this dilemma comes not from him, or if it comes from him, it does so in a curious way as the questions of a catechist drive him toward silence. In other poems where the speaker is engaged by an interlocutor ("Dialogue," "Love-unknown") there is a sense of genuine dialogue, of positions fully declared and patiently answered. Here the catechist wants to cut dialogue short. Arnold Stein suggests a comparison with the speeches of Christ in *Paradise Regained*, "accurate and concise, going to the heart of the matter without verbal cleverness" (p. 193n.), and I would extend the comparison to include Christ's brusqueness, his dismissal as so much ephemera of everything that is beside his point. Helen Vendler characterizes Love's "You shall be he," as "gentle,"[71] but I think she falls in too easily with the speaker's initial misreading of his own situation. He tells us that his host is "sweetly questioning," but the sweetness is heard only indirectly, in the report of Love's welcoming questions ("If I lacked anything"). "You shall be he" is the first instance in the poem of direct speech, and while the words are gracious in an ultimate (that is, theological) sense, they are not gentle, but peremptory. They do not mean either that the speaker *is* worthy, or that he shall be in the future, but that he is *declared* worthy. The statement is, as Stein says, "astounding" (p.

71. *The Poetry of George Herbert* (Cambridge, Mass., 1975), p. 275.

192), and not least because it does not even give the extended lament of "Dialogue" ("I can see no merit,/ Leading to this favour") a hearing. The question of merit is not adjudicated; it is simply set aside. Merit is not attributed to the speaker, nor is he found to be without it; rather, he is told that its determination has been made without reference to his deserts. "You shall be he" does not at all touch on the matter of whether or not he *should* be he. On its face, the statement seems generous, and in some final perspective it *is* generous; but in terms of what the speaker desires—an earned place—it is hard and unyielding because it denies him any part in the disposition of his own case.

In what follows, he is denied even more:

> I the unkinde, ungratefull? Ah my deare,
> > I cannot look on thee.
> Love took my hand, and smiling did reply,
> > Who made the eyes but I?

Love's smile is like his sweetness; it sugars a bitter pill. The speaker would like to be able to say "I'm not worthy even to look at you," but he is in effect told that he has no choice: if God creates and sustains everything, including the eyes, then one cannot but look on Him, if only because one looks with (by the agency of) Him. "Who made the eyes but I" (a variation of the familiar catechistical question) means "you cannot escape me because you are of my substance," and it has the effect of leaving the speaker with nothing to call his own. As a last resort, he lays claim to his guilt: "let my shame / Go where it doth deserve." Behind the shame, one hears the plea, let me at least have this; but Love is inexorable and asserts his title: "And know you not, sayes Love, who bore the blame?"

No sweetness or smiling disguises this preempting question; it is simply "said." The speaker capitulates, but asks for the mercy of dignity in defeat: "Then I will serve." But his opponent demands unconditional surrender: "You must sit down, sayes Love, and taste my meat." The strain of maintaining the fiction of a reciprocal exchange is felt most strongly in the modal "must" which has two readings: in ordinary social usage "must" does not carry the force of an imposed obligation; instead it is the politest of forms, as in "You must try some of my cheese-puffs"; but here the polite form is the thinnest of coverings for the naked command, in part because the word occurs at the end of a conversation in which the offer being made has been made again and again. It is as if your hostess were to entreat you for the fifth or sixth time; you might begin to suspect that it's an offer you can't refuse.

At any rate, the speaker of "Love III" does not refuse it:

> So I did sit and eat.

In Vendler's reading, the speaker "in sitting down in silent grateful acquiescence, attains at last the perfect simplicity that Love has displayed throughout" (p. 275), but the silence has been forced (he has spent his verbal resources) and gratitude is what he has been all along reluctant to give.[72] It is the kind of gratitude that is hardest to feel because it is for an action so complete that it leaves the beneficiary with nothing to do but accept, and even that action is not willed ("attains" is exactly the wrong verb) but made, by the giver, inescapable. The speaker's "So" is not triumphant, but exhausted: "What else could I do but what I had been told? So I did sit and

---

72. On this point, see Stein, *George Herbert's Lyrics*, p. 194.

eat." What he had been told was "do ye this in remembrance of me" and here in the face of Love's rigorous compassion he learns how that line is to be read: do this in remembrance of *me*, not of what you have done or would do ("I threatened to observe the strict decree / Of my deare God with all my power & might"),[73] but of what I have *already* done, and still do in every motion— including even the motion of sin—you would like to call your own. It is the lesson of the catechism:

Q. Do our works deserve nothing at Gods hand?
A. No: for they are his own works in us.[74]

This is devastating in its spareness, but in the catechism its force is diluted by the thousands of words that follow. The insight that one can do nothing is not likely to be confronted directly when someone is patiently and at length telling you what to do. In "Love III" that insight is inescapable, in part because the speaker tries for a time to escape it by pretending that he is a principal in a "contest of courtesy."[75] He loses the contest (he never had a chance) and with it his independent will. This, of course, is the goal of the Christian life ("In him we live and move and have our being"), but in this poem Herbert chooses to emphasize the price we pay for it, the price of knowing that it has been paid for by another. Vendler says that "during the actual progress of the poem," the distance between God and the soul "shrinks" (p. 274). In a way this is true, but the process is less comfortably benevolent than she implies because what shrinks or is shrunk is the speaker's self. He has been killed with kindness.

73. "The Holdfast," lines 1–2.
74. Egerton, *A briefe methode*, p. 11. See also Nowell, *A Catechism*, ed. Corrie, pp. 176–182, 199–200, 208–209, 216–217.
75. Stein, *George Herbert's Lyrics*, p. 194.

To the extent that this reading of "Love III" differs from most others it is because criticism has given us the poem we expect and, indeed, desire to find at the conclusion of "The Church." That poem, we feel, should be climactic and retrospective, recalling and resolving the conflicts that have previously been introduced and explored. In the reading proposed here, "Love III," rather than resolving conflicts, re-enacts them and confirms their durability. It could hardly be otherwise given the self-perpetuating rhythms of self-examination. The exercise of preparing to become worthy does not end in becoming worthy, but in the realization (stumbled upon again and again) that you never can be. It is an exercise that has no natural cessation; it cannot conclude, it can only be stopped by something outside its sphere. Here it is stopped by the very agent whose original act ("do ye this in remembrance of me") makes its goal unattainable, by a Questionist who does not say, "Congratulations, you've passed," but rather, "You still haven't got it right and never will, but come in and sit down anyway." It is easy to see why many readers (including this one) would like it otherwise, would like to reach a "plateau of assurance" and feel some measure of personal satisfaction at having attained it (along with the speaker) after so many false starts and defeated expectations. This is not to say that "Love III" communicates no sense of closure, but that it is a closure which, rather than being earned, is imposed. Insofar as we know that and know too that this tasting of "the churches mysticall repast" is only preliminary to another siege of doubts and questions, we will have been driven to another deep and dark point of religion.

Four: The Mystery of
The Temple Explained

1. THE CHURCH MILITANT

A NEW interpretation, like any other theory, should have at least two advantages over its predecessors: it should be simpler (here the criterion is one of "elegance") and it should explain more. Although it has taken many pages to present this interpretation, I believe it to be simpler because it rests on the recovery of a single tradition. That tradition has the advantage of allowing us to propose a reading of Herbert's title without detaching the sequence from the rich network of associations to which that title reaches out. One can assert that the primary reference is to the temple into which the reader is growing in the course of catechistical instruction and still maintain that it is a reference to the whole body of believers (the Church Militant) or to the perfect body of which those believers are members (living stones), or to the physical temple in which those members are made and confirmed (by the sacraments),[1] or to the body of poetry itself, which, insofar as it rests on the foundation of Christ, the cornerstone, rises into a temple.

The catechistical tradition is at once flexible enough to accommodate these significances and firm enough so that they are held in place by the controlling image of the progress of the catechumen through the stages of his edification, that is, of his building. Moreover, because the tradition is so flexible, there is a place in it for each of Herbert's interpreters. It is perfectly consistent with the reading proposed here to argue, as Joseph Summers does, that "it was the life of man within [the] Church which formed the principle of organization of Herbert's volume," although I would now add that the organization itself has an organization.[2] Nor is Martz wrong to claim that the same volume "grows" from the sacrament of the Holy Supper, although the growth is both more and less patterned than he seems to think it.[3] This new interpretation also gives comfort to those who would tie the order of the poems to the liturgical year, and it also explains why the emphasis falls so heavily on the feasts immediately preceding and following Easter, the forty-day period during which the catechumens prepared for the ceremonies of baptism and first communion. As Brewster Ford has shown, "the sequence . . . is closely

---

1. The catechisms teach that it is through the sacraments that we become members of the body of Christ. See, for example, Nowell, *A Catechisme* (1593), sig. f5^v: "We are by baptism received into the Church, and assured that we are now children of God, and joined and grafted into the bodie of Christ, and become his members, and do grow into one bodie with him." Nowell cites Ephesians 2:19–20, thus linking the sacrament with the building of the temple.

2. *George Herbert*, p. 87.

3. *The Poetry of Meditation*, p. 309.

and . . . purposely linked by Herbert to the succession of acts and states, objective and subjective, which lead the Christian from Baptism through human error into new grace in the Holy Communion. It is a sequence at once liturgical and chronological, at once sacramental and catechistic.''[4] It is not, however, architectural, at least not in the narrowly literal sense proposed by John David Walker.[5] Walker argues for a rather literal and sustained relationship between the furniture of the Temple in Jerusalem, the figurative significances attached to that furniture through centuries of exegesis, and the order of Herbert's poems. However, the correspondences he suggests have been resisted, largely because, as Annabel Endicott points out, "there is no obvious architectural order of precedence to the poems in 'The Church.'"[6] In this connection, "The Altar," for whose position Walker presents an elaborate explanation (pp. 294–295), poses a particular problem, for as Mary Rickey reminds us, "In no Christian Church . . . does one find this fixture immediately inside the entrance, and upon reading the 'Superliminare' one has figuratively gone through the door."[7] If, however, the order is seen not as (narrowly) architectural, but as catechistical, then the positioning of "The Altar" makes perfect sense: it follows poems whose experience prepares us to approach it. In the sequence of catechistical instruction one comes to the altar only after a thorough indoctrination in the moral knowledge offered by "The Church-porch" and after being made aware, as we are in "Superliminare," that such knowledge is not

4. *The Influence of The Prayer Book*, p. 132.
5. "The Architectonics of George Herbert's *The Temple*," pp. 289–305.
6. "The Structure of George Herbert's *Temple*," p. 234.
7. *Utmost Art*, pp. 10–11.

enough. Herbert is not Christopher Harvey; he is not interested in the Church and its furniture as occasions for allegorizing (although he does write some poems in that mode), but as stations along the road to a progress that is at once educational and liturgical. It is in relation to that (catechistical) road and not to any attempted architectural verisimilitude that "The Altar" appears where and when it does.

The significance of "The Altar['s]" position is only one of the problems that the introduction of the catechistical context is able to solve. Critics have tended to vacillate between a spatial and a temporal reading of the title, but it is now possible to assert both: the central action of the sequence is the growth of the reader-pupil into a living temple, but the living temple into which he grows already stands; it receives no addition from him, but incorporates him into membership. At any single point, the emphasis may be on one or the other, on the striving of the individual to find a place in the eternal order (to become a living stone), or on the priority of that order which is responsible for all the efforts of individuals to join it. The two perspectives are not in competition or contradictory; rather they co-exist in the same necessary and energy-creating tension that is found everywhere in the catechistical tradition (work to be done/work already done).

That same tradition explains much smaller problems. Of the poems in *The Temple*, few have received less attention than "The Jews": Martz, Summers, Stein, and Vendler do not even list it in their indexes, and, given the critical silence, one might wonder why the poem is in the sequence at all. The explanation is that the question asked by the poem—how and when will the Jews be reconciled with the Church—is one that has a ready-made answer in what I have called the rhetoric of templehood. The key is the word "cornerstone" as it is found both in the commentaries on Peter and Ephesians and in the catechisms which take so many of their arguments and images from those texts. The cornerstone is, of course, Jesus Christ ("Jesus Christ himself being the chief cornerstone"), and the list of his unifying properties always includes the ability to bring together Christians and Jews in the temple of which he is at once foundation, material, body, and builder. "He is well said to be Head of the corner," explains Nicholas Byfield, "because upon Christ meet (as the two sides meete in the cornerstone) both Angels and men; and amongst men, both the Saints in heaven, and the godly on earth; and amongst men on earth, both Jewes and Gentiles."[8] Niels Hemmingsen makes the same (commonplace) point and elaborates on it: "For, as the cornerstone joineth walles together, and beareth up the whole burthen of the building: yea, preserveth it: even so our Lord Jesus Christ . . . knitteth the Jewes and the Gentiles in unitie of Faith and peace: and so he himselfe upholdeth and maintaineth this spirituall building."[9] As a cornerstone, Augustine observes, Christ fulfills the prophecy of Isaiah ("thus saith the Lord . . . Behold I lay in Zion for a foundation a stone, a tried stone, a precious corner stone") whose wish it was that in him "both classes coming together as walls from different sides, that is to say from the Jews and the Gentiles, might be joined in genuine love."[10] It is for such a joining that the speaker of "The Jewes" petitions, al-

8. *A commentary; or sermons,* pp. 246–247.
9. *The Epistle of the Blessed Apostle,* p. 97.
10. *De Catechizandis Rudibus,* ed. Christopher, p. 75.

though he doubts that his own prayers will be sufficient to effect it: "Oh that my prayers! mine, alas!/ Oh that some Angel might a trumpet sound" (lines 7–8). He ends as he began, lamenting the breach between the two peoples, and hoping that his "deare Lord" will be moved to repair it. But the reader who knows the history of the poem's topos will also know that the wished-for reconciliation has already been achieved because "this spirituall building," with its firmly cementing cornerstone, already stands. The lesson of the poem (and of many others) is given in "Prayer II"—"We cannot ask the thing, which is not there" (line 11)—and it is a lesson that directs us to one more way in which the work to be done has been done already.

By thus reestablishing the context in which it is to be read, it becomes possible to relate "The Jews" to the sequence and its concerns. To be sure, the success is a small one (and is not likely to enhance the reputation of the poem), but together with the larger successes I have been claiming, it is one more testimony to the explanatory power of this interpretation. One of the more important things it explains is "The Church Militant." The argument for the unity of *The Temple* has more often than not foundered on the question of this long poem. It presents two large problems. The first concerns Herbert's intentions, which remain obscure. In both the Bodleian and the Williams manuscripts, "The Church Militant" stands apart from the previous poems, separated in one by a blank page and in the other by five blank pages. Moreover, according to Hutchinson, "all the internal evidence points to an early date for the inception of this poem" (p. 543). He speculates that "Herbert perhaps came to recognize that his lyrical gift was not well fitted

for ambitious attempts of this kind," and Annabel Endicott takes his speculation to its logical conclusion: "It
would seem wiser not to force the third poem into the
structure of *The Temple*, but to see it simply as an earlier
work included there for convenience."[11] These arguments are based on the assumption that Herbert's intentions cannot be inferred from the first edition, but that
assumption has recently been challenged by J. Max Patrick who believes that "there is far more reason for accepting the editions of 1633 as realizing Herbert's intention than for granting higher verbal authority to the
manuscript made for the licencers."[12]

Of course, even if it were proved that Herbert intended
to integrate "The Church Militant" into *The Temple*, we
would still be free to decide that he had failed. This is, in
fact, the second problem presented by the poem: it does
not seem to be a fit conclusion to the poems that precede
it. First of all, it is obviously different in form: the poems
of the first two sections, says Lee Ann Johnson, "form a
harmonious whole by virtue of their subjectivity, tone,
and emotion." That is, they are what "one would expect
to find in a volume described by its author as 'a picture of
the many spiritual Conflicts that have past betwixt God
and my Soul.'" "The Church Militant," however, is not a
lyric, but "a long, five-part narrative of the westward
movement of the Church with the parallel advance of
'Sinne.'"[13] That advance is relentless and results in a
sombreness of tone that is an obstacle in the way of those
who require the sequence to end confidently. Stanley

11. "Structure of Herbert's *Temple*," p. 236.
12. "Critical Problems in Editing George Herbert's *The Temple*," p. 13.
13. "The Relationship of 'The Church Militant' to *The Temple*," *SP*, 68
(1971), p. 201.

Stewart is eloquent in proposing that as an apocalyptic
poem, "a poem concerned, not with the struggle of the
soul in time, but with the movement of the Church
throughout all time," "The Church Militant" is properly
"detached and austere";[14] but one must finally agree
when Johnson demurs: the poem simply "does not reflect the optimism which Stewart implies" (p. 204). Endicott makes a similar objection to Walker's thesis that
"The Church Militant" is to be identified with the holy of
holies in the Temple of Jerusalem, and represents "the
climactic end of the soul's progress from earth to heaven"
(pp. 304–305); if Herbert had such a plan in mind, she
reasons, surely he would have called his holy of holies
"The Church Triumphant" instead of "The Church
Militant," especially since the distinction between the
two is precisely between the good and the perfect, the
partial and the complete.[15]

Perfect, complete, and climactic is what many readers
would like *The Temple* to be, but "The Church Militant,"
pessimistic, inconclusive, and anticlimactic, is an imped-
iment that those same readers feel obliged either to dis-
tort or remove. Again it is the catechistical tradition that
allows us to resolve an impasse by providing a context for
the poem as it is rather than as we might wish it to be. In
that tradition, as we have seen, membership in The
Church Militant stands as the goal of the initiatory rites
that begin with the prebaptismal instructions on the
church porch. It is one of the temples that catechizing
builds up, living stone by living stone. Immanuel Bourne
ends his "Epistle Dedicatory" by praying that "by the

14. "Time and *The Temple*," *SEL*, 6 (1966), p. 201.
15. "The Structure of George Herbert's *Temple*," pp. 230, 236.

help of this or my lesser Catechism . . . your souls and several Families . . . may be enlightened . . . by the true light of Christ in the Church Militant";[16] and J. F. reminds us that in the early liturgy "instruction in the principles of Religion" continued all the year until the "strangers from the covenant" were "admitted into the societie of the Saints."[17] As O. B. Hardison observes, the entire Easter drama leads up to this moment, which occurs immediately after the second approach to the altar: "On Sunday after Easter the neophytes remove their white robes. This act symbolizes both the final repose of the blessed and the entry of the neophytes into the ranks of the Church Militant."[18]

It makes perfect and even predictable sense, then, for Herbert to give the last section of *The Temple* a title that links it to the final stage of the sequence he has chosen for a model. The link is made even firmer by the content of the poem, which corresponds perfectly to a standard feature of the early catechisms, the *narratio* or "history of salvation" as it is embodied in the career of the Church. The earliest known example of this practice is the *Demonstratio praeficationis Apostolorum* of Irenaeus, of which the *narratio* is fully one half. It begins with the creation of the world and comes to a climax with the birth of Christ, who in his person is said to sum up all things, "those of Heaven and those of this earth."[19] As Daniélou notes, Christ provides the continuity to the narration, for every

16. *A light from Christ*, sig. A6^v.

17. *The Covenant betweene God And Man*, pp. 60–61.

18. O.B. Hardison, Jr., *Christian Rite and Christian Drama in the Middle Ages* (Baltimore, 1965), p. 175.

19. *Démonstration de la Prédication Apostolique*, ed. and trans. L. M. Froidevaux (Paris, 1959), p. 80. On the subject of the *narratio*, see Daniélou, *La Catéchèse Aux Premiers Siècles*, pp. 27, 28, 90–102, 249–262.

event in it looks forward to the Incarnation. ("Il y a con-
tinuité de la présence du Verbe, depuis les origines
jusqu'à l'Incarnation.") The actions of men are continually being referred to the agency of God, and the result is
a totally unified history, "celui du dessin de Dieu ab-
solument un, de la création à la rédemption."[20] Creation
and redemption are also the beginning and end points of
the *narratio*, whose outlines are given in the *Apostolical
Constitutions* (once thought to be Clement's, but now
usually assigned to the fourth century):

Let [the catechumen] learn the order of the several parts of
creation. . . . Let him be instructed why the world was
made. . . . Let him be taught how God punished the wicked
with water and fire, and did glorify the saints in every
generation—I mean Seth, and Enos, and Enoch, and Noah,
and Abraham, and his posterity, and Melchizedek, and Job,
and Moses, and Joshua, and Caleb, and Phineas the priest, and
those that were holy in every generation. . . . Let him that offers himself to baptism learn these and the like things during
the time that he is a catechumen; and let him . . . adore God,
the Lord of the whole world, and thank Him for His creation,
for His sending Christ His only begotten Son, that he might
save man by blotting out his transgressions.[21]

By the fourth century, the *narratio* is an established part of
the catechism, and in Etheria's account of the catechizing
of the candidates for baptism it figures prominently:

. . . the chair is placed for the Bishop at the Martyrium in the
great church, and all who are to be baptized sit around. . . . Be-
sides these, all the people who wish to hear come in and sit
down—the faithful however only, for no catechumen enters
there when the Bishop teaches the others the law. Beginning

20. *Ibid.*, pp. 93, 91.
21. *The Apostolical Constitutions*, in *Ante-Nicene Christian Library*, vol.
17, ed. Rev. A. Roberts and J. Donaldson (Edinburgh, 1870), p. 200.

from Genesis he goes through all the scriptures during those forty days, explaining them, first literally, and then unfolding them spiritually. They are also taught about the Resurrection, and likewise all things concerning the Faith during those days. And this is called the catechising. (p. 574)

The same sequence was enacted in the night of the Easter Vigil when selected texts from the Old Testament were read and expounded. These readings might vary, both in number and content, but their purpose was always the same, to instruct the assembled candidates in "the history of creation, the history of the Fall and the promise of redemption."[22]

It was Augustine who brought the *narratio* to its full development by including in his chronicle not only biblical history, but the history of the Church down to his own time (p. 5). The *De Catechizandis Rudibus* was written in answer to Deogratias, a deacon of Carthage, who had asked Augustine for advice on how to manage the business of catechizing, "how suitably to present that truth the belief in which makes us Christians; where to begin the *narratio*, to what point it should be brought down, and whether at the close of the *narratio* an examination should be added or precept only" (p. 13). As Reverend Christopher points out, the fact that the two correspondents use the term *narratio* so easily is one indication of its established place in the catechism (p. 95). In Augustine's practice, as he reports it to Deogratias, the *narratio* follows an inquiry into the candidate's motives for desiring to become a Christian. Once the catechist is satisfied that the candidate has not "come with a counterfeit motive,

22. Philip Weller, ed., *The Easter Sermons of St. Augustine* (Washington, 1955), p. 45. See also Hardison, *Christian Rite*, pp. 149ff.

desirous only of temporal advantages" (p. 25), the *narratio* should begin,

starting out from the fact that God made all things very good, and continuing . . . down to the present period of Church history, in such a way as to account for and explain the causes and reasons of each of the facts and events that we relate, and thereby refer them to that end of love from which in all our actions and words our eyes should never be turned away. (pp. 26–27)

That narrative proper is divided into six ages corresponding, says Augustine, to the six days of creation.[23]

The first is from the beginning of the human race . . . to Noe. . . . The second extends from that point to Abraham. . . . The third age is from Abraham down to King David; the fourth, from David down to that captivity in which God's people migrated to Babylon; the fifth, from that migration down to the coming of our Lord Jesus Christ. From His coming the sixth age is dated. (p. 70)

The sixth is the age in which we still live; its duration is uncertain and its end will coincide with the inauguration of the seventh when "He would be at rest in His saints, because they themselves will rest in Him after all the good works wherein they have served Him" (p. 57). Meanwhile, however, there is no rest, only the long and outwardly unhappy history of the Church in which "many consent to the devil, and few follow God" (p. 60). Like Milton after him, Augustine contrasts the multitudes of the wicked with the "one just man" who periodically appears to maintain the ways of the City of God. Noah may save the human race in the Ark, but "even after this wickedness did not cease to sprout forth

23. On this point, see Christopher's note, *De Catechizandis*, pp. 123–124.

again through pride and lust" (p. 62). Once again, almost all nations "served idols and evil spirits," but there were "also a few who thought on the rest to come and sought a heavenly home" (p. 63). The sequence is repeated in the time of Moses when the Jews who receive the Law do not understand it; the stone tablets "typify the hardness of their hearts . . . inasmuch as . . . they were held more by carnal fear than by spiritual love" (p. 65). Of course the spiritual significances of the Law's ordinances were "understood by a few holy men," but by "the multitude of carnal men they were observed only, not understood" (p. 66).

The point of the catechistical instruction is to prepare the candidate to become one of those "holy few," and it is important that he understand that the road to be traveled is a long and difficult one. Triumph may await in the seventh age, but now, in this life and in history, the holy man's lot is "more grievous and more frequent persecutions," fulfilling the word "that the Lord had foretold: *Behold I send you as sheep in the midst of wolves*" (p. 75). Even this, however, can be understood as a part of God's plan for the faithful: as the "vine" that is the Church spreads "its branches throughout the world," it must be periodically "pruned . . . that from it should be lopped the unfruitful branches . . . by which . . . heresies and schisms were occasioned . . . on the part of those who sought not His glory but their own, so that through their opposition the Church might be more and more tried, and both her teaching elucidated and her long-suffering tested" (p. 76). This, then, is the promise, but for the most part the emphasis falls on the "long-suffering" and on the proliferation of "schisms and heresies" (p. 85). What remains to the members of the true Church, of the

Church Militant, is hope and the anticipation of "the day of judgment which shall separate all the wicked from the good in the resurrection of the dead, and shall set apart for the fire . . . not only those without the Church, but also the chaff of the Church herself, which she must bear with utmost patience until the final winnowing" (p. 85). The theme of the final winnowing or last judgment is the end of the *narratio* as it is the end of history: "At the conclusion of the *narratio* we should make known to him [the candidate] the hope in the resurrection . . . and speak to him of the last judgment to come, with its goodness towards the good and its severity towards the wicked, its certainty in relation to all" (pp. 27–28). It is on this day that the two cities which have "from the beginning of the human race" been "intermingled" will finally be separated (p. 61), as "all the citizens of both these cities shall receive again their bodies and rise and shall render an account of their life before the judgment seat of Christ, the Judge" (p. 76).

This is precisely how Herbert's "Church Militant" ends, with the Church and Sin making their entangled way together toward the time and place of the last judgment:

Yet as the Church shall thither westward flie,
So Sinne shall trace and dog her instantly:
They have their period also and set times
Both for their vertuous actions and their crimes.
And where of old the Empire and the Arts
Usher'd the Gospel ever in mens hearts,
Spain hath done one; when Arts perform the other,
The Church shall come, & Sinne the Church shall smother:
That when they have accomplished their round,
And met in th' east their first and ancient sound,
Judgement may meet them both & search them round.

> Thus do both lights, as well in Church as Sunne,
> Light one another, and together runne.
> Thus also Sinne and Darknesse follow still
> The Church and Sunne with all their power and skill.
> But as the Sunne still goes both west and east;
> So also did the Church by going west
> Still eastward go; because it drew more neare
> To time and place, where judgement shall appeare.
> *Now deare to me, O God, thy counsels are!*
> *Who may with thee compare?*

(lines 259–279)

The refrain (lines 278–279) is resonant of confidence and faith, but it exists in an ever-increasing state of tension with the narrative it punctuates, a dreary chronicle in which sin repeatedly triumphs and the members of the true Church "decrease and fade" (lines 211, 229). That chronicle does not end, but stops, offering less and less support for the speaker's periodic affirmations. If history is a trial for the long-suffering faithful, then the history rehearsed here is a trial for the long-suffering reader, who is asked to approve the refrain in the face of the overwhelming evidence for a quite different conclusion. In this way, the poem becomes a test of the reader's faith, of his resolve to continue believing and by so continuing to renew his membership in the Church Militant.

Obviously, then, "The Church Militant" is Herbert's *narratio*, answerable in every way to the traditional formula. All its events are referred to one final cause, the love of God: "Thy Church and Spouse prove/ Not the decrees of power, but bands of love" (lines 9–10). As in Augustine, the principal actor is the Church, characterized as a vine—"Early didst thou arise to plant this vine / Which might the more indeare it to be thine" (lines 11–12)—whose diseased branches must repeatedly be pruned. The major difference between the two *narratios* only underlines Herbert's fidelity to the conventions of the form. In the sample catechism of the *De Catechizandis Rudibus*, the emphasis falls on the five ages leading up to the birth of Christ; but in "The Church Militant" Christ has already been born by line 25, and it is the sixth age, the history of the Church down to the present time, that occupies the remainder of the poem. These proportions should not be surprising; they merely testify to the fact that more than 1200 years have passed since Augustine wrote and there is that much more of the Church's "long-suffering" to record. One might also say that this is a distinctly Protestant *narratio*. Sin enjoys his greatest triumph at Rome where he "bravely resolv'd one night / To be a Churchman too, and wear a Mitre" (lines 162–163). His imposture is so successful that "he carri'd all mens eyes,/ While Truth sat by" (lines 189–190). The whole world "did seem but the Popes mule" (line 204) as "Sinne triumphs in Western *Babylon*, yet not as Sinne, but as Religion" (lines 211–212). Of course the very recent past has witnessed a reformation, but it is a case of too little too late: "The second Temple could not reach the first: / And the late reformation never durst / Compare with ancient times and purer yeares" (lines 225–227). Religion continues to flee westward as the history breaks off and the faithful are left to await a darkness so total that only the light of the second coming (whose imminence it announces) will be able to dispel it: "Till such a darknesse do the world invade/ At Christs last coming, as his first did finde" (lines 230–231).

As he is in so many other respects, Herbert is unique in his addition of a *narratio* to the catechistical sequence. Only Andrewes among the Reformation catechists I have read includes so much historical material, but his history comes in bits and pieces and does not take the form of a sustained chronicle. Fortunately, we can with some confidence assume that Herbert's source is Augustine himself. We know from the poet's will that his library included "St. Augustines workes,"[24] and it is certain that his lifelong interest in catechizing would have led him to study the *De Catechizandis Rudibus* closely. It is likely that Augustine's influence is also at least partly responsible for the other unique feature of Herbert's catechistical theory and practice, his varying of the questions according to the capacity of the pupil so that he might play a part in his own edification. The *De Catechizandis Rudibus* is, according to Reverend Christopher, "the first treatise on catechesis in which the pedagogical value of suggestive questions . . . is brought out" (p. 117). Like Herbert, Augustine urges the catechist to proceed with joy and enthusiasm so that what is old to him "may grow interesting because of our hearers for whom it is all new" (p. 42). Those hearers will bring with them different abilities and problems and it will be necessary to pursue a different strategy with each candidate in order to bring him to discover what he is:

We must in our discourse make trial of everything that may succeed in rousing him. . . . We must drive out by gentle encouragement his excessive timidity, which hinders him from expressing his opinion. . . . We must by questioning him find out whether he understands; and must give him confidence so that if he thinks there is an objection to make he may freely lay it before us. We must at the same time enquire of him whether he has ever heard these things before. . . . We must then act in accordance with his answer, so as either to speak more clearly

24. Hutchinson, *Works of George Herbert,* p. 152.

or simply, or to refute a contrary opinion, or not to set forth at greater length things that are familiar to him. (p. 43).
I am differently stirred according as he whom I see before me waiting for instruction is cultivated or a dullard, a fellow citizen or a stranger, a rich man or a poor man, . . . a person of this or that family, of this or that age or sex, coming to us from this or that school of philosophy, or from this or that popular error; and in keeping with my own varying feelings my discourse itself opens, proceeds, and closes, and since the same medicine is not to be applied to all, although to all the same love is due, so also love itself is in travail with some, becomes weak with others; is at pains to edify some, dreads to be a cause of offense to others; stoops to some, before others stands with head erect; is gentle to some, and stern to others; and enemy to none, a mother to all. (pp. 50–51)

This is the same love to which all the events in the *narratio* are to be referred. History is the record of those who have known this love and who have through it become members of the Church Militant; and it is through the catechism, also informed by love, that new members are even now being added:

For behold, we too are now building up and planting you by this discourse. And this is being done throughout the whole world . . . even as the . . . apostle says: *You are God's husbandry, God's building.* (p. 69)

2. THE AESTHETIC OF THE UNFINISHED

The fact that we are now able to place "The Church Militant" in the tradition that served as Herbert's model does not constitute an answer to its critics. The poem is still inconclusive, ill-proportioned, and anticlimactic, and it does not leave the reader with a satisfactory sense of closure. Nor is it meant to. The very idea of the Church Militant has at its heart the necessity of struggle and toil:

"The militant Church here on earth, hath no certaine place, but is posted from piller to post."[25] Rest and closure are unavailable except in some premature and therefore dangerous assumption that God's building is already finished. It is a danger against which one must constantly be on guard. "While a house is not fully built," declares Paul Baynes, "the workmen may not be dismissed; and until the house of God have every beleever, every stone of it laid, the builders of it must be continued."[26] Not only must the ministers and catechizers continue their work, but every believer must be continually worked on: "Before a rough stone can be commodiously laid, it must be hewed by the Mason, fitted, polished and plained, and so brought to the rest of the building; so it is with you, you must be smoothed and plained, before you can come to lye in this building" (p. 325). "Even as it is in great buildings, they are not at once begunne and perfected: So it is, the whole and every living stone have their increase till they come to perfection" (p. 326). Perfection, however, will never be attained, at least not in this life: "The stones of the temple were hewed in Lebanon, till they were fit to bee transported to the temple: So we must never leave these

25. Robert Cawdrey, *A treasurie or store-house of similes* (1600), pp. 93–94. Quoted by Barbara Lewalski, "Typology and Poetry: A Consideration of Herbert, Vaughan, and Marvell," in *Illustrious Evidence: Approaches to English Literature of the Early Seventeenth Century* (Berkeley and Los Angeles, 1975), p. 53. Professor Lewalski comments: "Herbert's perception is that the Temple, with its intimations of permanence, has its true antitype only in the hearts of the elect who look forward to individual salvation, but that the wandering Ark is the nearest type for the corporate body of the Church, which has no security here and is (as Augustine also saw) in constant conflict with the world."

26. *A Commentary upon the Epistle*, p. 492.

builders, till we are fitted and translated hence to heaven." "Doubtless," says Chrysostom, "this is a building that shall go on until his coming."[27] Thus, explains Samuel Lee, "the Gospel-Ministry . . . must endure till all the Elect be gathered and built up into a holy Temple in the Lord, which shall not be fully and compleatly finished till the end of the World."[28] Those who wish it otherwise, who think to have their rest and reward here and now "stumble at that which is the unavoidable condition of the Church Militant, and would have heaven on earth, a perfect unity before we all meet."[29]

Those readers who wish that "The Church Militant" were other than it is make the same mistake. Endicott is surely right to object that the defenders of the poem argue as if it were entitled "The Church Triumphant," but she is wrong, I think, to conclude that it has no place in "the structure of *The Temple*" (p. 236). For were we to leave *The Temple* with a sense of peace and security, then Herbert would have failed of his obligation as a teacher-catechist, which is to inure his reader-pupils to the patience that is the lot of those who labor in the service of God. "But have the Saints of God no Vacation? doe they never cease?" asks Donne, and the answer is immediate and unequivocal: "They have no *rest*. Beloved, God himselfe rested not, till the seventh day: be thou content to stay for thy sabbath, till thou maist have an eternall one, . . . so, howsoever God deale with thee, be not thou weary of bearing thy part, in his Quire, here in the Militant Church."[30] As readers of *The Temple* we must be

27. *Homilies*, ed. John Henry Parker (Oxford, 1845), p. 159.

28. *Orbis miraculum* (1659), p. 190.

29. Baynes, *A Commentary*, p. 493.

30. *The Sermons*, ed. George R. Potter and Evelyn M. Simpson (Berkeley and Los Angeles, 1953–1962), vol. VIII, pp. 52–53.

content to stay for our sabbath, if only because Herbert insists on withholding it from us now. Walker, Stewart, and others misread "The Church Militant" because they do not find in it what they want, the satisfaction of a resoundingly affirmative conclusion; but it is by refusing us that satisfaction, and by referring us to a future moment it can neither present nor contain, that the poem fulfills its function in the sequence.

One might say, then, that both as a poem and as an experience, *The Temple* is unfinished, and quite properly so. "In this life," Henry Ainsworth reminds us, "we are but in the growth . . . still growing . . . we in this house of God must be still in building."[31] "The builders," says Matthew Poole, "are still at work, and this Temple not yet finished,"[32] and "it will not be finished," Nicholas Byfield tells us, "till we be settled in that Building made without hands in heaven."[33] And yet in another sense, one that is captured in the ambiguity of Byfield's language, "this Temple" is already finished because that "building without hands" is already "made," not however by the builders who are here urged to continue in their work, but by the Builder whose work knows no time of beginning or ending because it is done (*all* the time) in eternity. "Made in heaven" is a label that takes the act of making out of time, and yet it is in time that those who are urged both to build and become temples must operate. Here once again we find the radical ambiguity that is at the very heart of the catechist's project: on the one hand he is told in no uncertain terms that there is work to be done, and on the other he is reminded no less forcefully that the work has already been done by another. As

31. *Certain notes*, sigs. B4ᵛ, B5ʳ.
32. *Annotations*, sig. Qqq3ʳ.
33. Byfield, *A Commentary; or sermons*, p. 196.

Heather Asals points out, this devaluation of the present in favor of a past that has assured the future is a familiar theme in the seventeenth century. She cites George Wither for a statement that has innumerable parallels in Milton and others:

For, although the mysteries of the Gospell . . . were not then fulfilled in act, in respect to us to whom they were to be manifested in *Time:* yet in regard to God, with whom all *Times* are present, they might be properly enough mentioned as things alreadie effected.[34]

Here is a precise formulation of our dilemma: if things are "alreadie effected," what are we to make of the command to effect them? How are we either to fashion or become living stones if the temple already stands? These same questions are asked by Herbert himself in a number of poems that directly confront the paradox of a temporal urgency that is ultimately an illusion. Often, the subject of these poems is the action they propose to perform: praise, thanksgiving, contrition, humility; and the insight they yield (or force) is that these actions have already been performed by Christ. "Weep not, deare friends, since I for both have wept," declares Christ in "The Sacrifice" (line 149), and this is only one of the ways in which both the poet and the reader find themselves "prevented." In "Providence" the speaker is able to acknowledge this preventing and even to celebrate it:

> We all acknowledge both thy power and love
> To be exact, transcendent, and divine;
> Who dost so strongly and so sweetly move,
> While all things have their will, yet none but thine.
>
> (lines 29–32)

34. "The Voice of George Herbert's 'The Church,'" *ELH,* 36 (1969), 525.

But in other poems, the acknowledgment comes harder. The speaker of "The Holdfast" announces a succession of resolutions, each of which is an attempt to claim for himself some small area of independent action, but in every instance he finds that God has reserved that area to himself ("ev'n to trust in him, was also his").[35] "How shall I grieve for thee?" cries the poet in "The Thanksgiving" as he rehearses a catalogue of the things he cannot (independently) do because they have already been done:

> Shall I weep bloud? why, thou hast wept such store
>   That all thy body was one doore.
> Shall I be scourged, flouted, boxed, sold?
>   'Tis but to tell the tale is told.
>
> (lines 5–8)

The tale that is already told includes the tale that he is now telling. He may complain, in "Temper I" and other poems, of God's fitful presence and apparent desertion, but that complaint has been definitively anticipated in all its particulars by the figure on the cross—"My God, my God, why hast thou forsaken mee?"—just as his recoveries ("bringing down to hell / And up to heaven in an houre")[36] have their circumscribing pattern in the resurrection. *The Temple* may be a "picture of the many spiritual conflicts that have past betwixt God and [his] soul," but it is a picture whose outlines and details are drawn before he comes to retrace them. Even his requests refer to favors that have already been granted: "We cannot ask the thing, which is not there" ("Prayer II," line 11). Nor can we write the thing that is not already written: "*There is in love a sweetnesse readie penn'd,*" declares the

---

35. For a full discussion, see *Self-Consuming Artifacts,* pp. 174–176.
36. "The Flower," lines 16–17.

friend in "Jordan II": "*Copie out onely that, and save ex-pense*" (lines 17–18). In this view everything is a copy of an original, a repetition in time and history of what is already done in eternity. There is only one story, and it "pennes and sets us down."[37]

It follows, then, that while action is necessary (it is continually urged in the scriptures, in sermons, in cate-chisms), the agent cannot claim credit for either its im-pulses or its effects. ("Let me not think an action mine own way," the poet petitions in "Obedience.") That is, one must do the best that one can while at the same time believing that, unaided, one can do nothing. It is a bal-ance almost impossible to achieve and the result is a situ-ation in which the agent has no room to maneuver. Whatever he does, he finds that God is always there before him with a prior claim. Any action he would take is, as Herbert says in "The Elixir," "prepossest" (line 7). The prefix makes my point: the act not only belongs to God, but it always has.

In the face of this realization, what is one to do? How can we obey the injunction to serve God, if his power and omnipresence join to make service impossible? Herbert's speakers typically answer these questions by resolving to act in such a way as to "resign up the rudder" to God's skill,[38] to refer everything that is done to him:

> He that does ought for thee,
> Marketh y^t deed for thine.[39]

But rather than removing the impasse, this strategy merely relocates it. One may resolve to so act as to make

37. "The Bunch of Grapes," line 11.
38. "Obedience," line 20.
39. Cancelled verse from "The Elixir." See Hutchinson, p. 184.

God "prepossest," but that resolution is no less his pre-possession than the actions it resigns. There is no way to stand outside the dilemma (indeed the wish to stand outside it defines one pole of its danger); one can only acknowledge it in gestures that are not themselves to be regarded as the spontaneous expressions of an independent will.

It is just such a gesture that Herbert makes when he concludes *The Temple* with the anticlimax of "The Church Militant" and thereby relinquishes any claim to have finished his work, in the sense either that it *is* finished or that *he* has finished it. His is a theological version of Bacon's secular strategy, an aesthetic of the unfinished, but with a difference: for while Bacon leaves his loose ends hanging so that those "who come after him" will not assume prematurely that the job has been done, Herbert would have us realize that the job can never be done, at least not by any human author. It is this realization that stands behind his studied unconcern with the finer points of the poet's art. His rhyme may be disordered (as in "Deniall"), but God will correct it; it may be inappropriate (as in "Home"), but God will change it; He will make the verse run smooth ("Sonnett" from Walton's *Lives*) or approve it even when it does not: "He will be pleased with that dittie;/ And if I please him, I write fine and wittie" ("The Forerunners," lines 11–12). Nothing the poet does will be wrong, not, however, because he is doing things right, but because in this fortunate universe God turns (indeed has already turned) all to good.[40] Even

40. Cf. Baynes, *A Commentary*, p. 332: "It may comfort us that wee shall in due time be finished; God will make up all the breaches and ruines of our sinfull nature, and build us up a glorious Temple for himselfe, wherein he will dwell for ever."

if the poet were to stop and leave his task incomplete, it would complete itself because in one important sense it was complete before he came to it:

> . . . if I chance to hold my peace,
> These stones to praise thee may not cease.
> ("The Altar," lines 13–14)

While the finishing of the altar (or poem or sequence of poems) is an enjoined labor, it is not one for which the agent need, or indeed can, take responsibility. He need not because the task is finished already, and he cannot because the credit for finishing it belongs solely to God. It is not simply that the poet can afford to leave his work imcomplete; it is incumbent upon him to leave it incomplete, lest he appear to be claiming for it, and therefore for himself, more than any human agency is allowed. It is a claim men are all too prone to make. *"We have the more need,"* says Anthony Burgesse, *"to exalt Christ, because there is pronenesse in every man to trust in his own works"* (p. 152). Herbert exalts Christ by relying on him to write the conclusion to "his own works." If *The Temple* is unfinished so that the reader will not be tempted to a false sense of security and achievement, the strategy is one that also protects the poet from the same danger.

It is a strategy Herbert could have learned from the catechists he follows. Augustine instructs Deogratias to instruct his pupil "against placing his hope in man" (p. 29), and in what follows he extends the warning to himself: "When he who is listening to us, or rather listening to God through us, begins to make progress in knowledge and morality . . . he will not venture to ascribe the change either to us or to himself." The *correctio (immo per nos audit deum)* is obviously self-protective; even the teacher of teachers must constantly remind himself of what he is *not* doing. *"Who was the first Author of this course,"* asks Gervase Babington and answers immediately: "The surest and safest Author to be followed in any thing, even GOD himself."[41] In John Boughton's catechism, Jacob (the persona of the catechist) asks the same question—"who was the author of this form of teaching?"—and receives from Benjamin the same answer: "Even God himself."[42] It is not I, declares William Crashaw, who lays "the foundation among you," but "Gods providence," for *"other foundation can not man lay than that that is already so well laid, even Jesus Christ."*[43] It was Christ who catechized Nicodemus[44] and the Samaritan woman,[45] and it is he who now speaks through the catechists of the present day, "being taught by his spirit."[46] Bourne promises "to hold forth in the Catechism following what Light I have received from Christ, to lead unto Christ."[47] Christ is not only the material to be taught, and the goal of the educational experience, he is also the

41. *Comfortable notes upon the bookes of Numbers and Deuteronomie* (1615), p. 205.

42. *God and man or a treatise catechisticall,* p. 1.

43. *Milke for babes, or a north-countrie catechisme* (1622), sig. A3ʳ.

44. See "A Discourse of Confirmation," in *The Whole Works of the Right Rev. Jeremy Taylor, D.D.,* vol. III, ed. F. Westley and A. H. Davis (London, 1835), p. 10: "Our blessed Saviour was catechising of Nicodemus, and teaching him the first rudiments of the gospel, and like a wise master-builder, first lays the foundation." Taylor goes on to give an account of the early history of catechizing, citing Cyril and Augustine, among others (pp. 29–30).

45. See Martin Bucer, *De Regno Christi,* in *The Library of Christian Classics,* vol. 19, ed. W. Pauck (Philadelphia, 1969), p. 235.

46. T.W., *An exposition,* p. 4.

47. *A light from Christ,* sig. A2ᵛ.

teacher; and in the prayer Daniel Featly sets before his catechism he is even the pupil:

Sit thou in the middest of us here assembled, as thou satest in the *middest of the Doctors in the Temple, opposing and answering them*. Propound such Questions by me, and returne such Answers by them, as may clearly expresse to our understanding, and imprint in our memories the necessary points of saving truth, and foundations of Christian Doctrine; and may serve for the instruction of the ignorant, admonition of the learned, and *the building up of us all in our most holy faith*. [48]

Andrewes concludes "as *Cyril* did his preface, *Meum est docere. Vestrum auscultare. Dei perficere.*"[49] After calling his pupils "the seed plot of heaven," John Jewel exhorts, "Let us water them that God may give the increase."[50] Samuel Hieron sums it all up in the closing words of his catechism: *"Let God alone have the glory."*[51]

To do otherwise, to catechize in a way that would not make God prepossessed, would be to build the temple on the rotten foundation of the self: Burgesse warns that "whosoever builds his salvation upon his parts, his duties, . . . his enlargements . . . this mans foundation is self."[52] It is God "who makes . . . this glorious building," for men by their own power "could never become a fit habitation for the Lord to rest in. We are not born but made the house and building of God" (p. 118). Although at several points in the Scriptures it is the apostles who are called the foundation, "the Apostles are only *foundations* that are built upon another foundation, *viz. Christ*" (p. 145); "when men are not built on Christs Doctrine, but

48. *The summe of saving knowledge* (1626).
49. *A patterne*, p. 13.
50. *Works*, vol. VIII, p. 51.
51. *The doctrine of the beginning of Christ* (1620), sig. C7ʳ.
52. *The Scripture directory*, p. 136.

their own opinions, their own conceits, they have *Reubens* curse, *unstable like water*" (p. 155). The Papists may claim that first Peter and now the Pope are the foundations, but "the foundation on which we are laid, is the same on which the prophets builded: the Prophets builded not on the Pope."[53] The word is unrelenting in its claims: "None can be a foundation properly bearing up, but Christ; for it is the spirit of Faith comming from him which doth uphold us." "*It is the vertue of God our Lord which doth build up* . . . not the strength of men" (p. 331).

This is not merely a lesson that catechists teach, but one they must constantly apply to the teaching they do. The catechist may exhort his pupils, "you must be smoothed and plained, before you can come to lye in this building,"[54] but he no less than they is undergoing the same smoothing and planing. As a builder he must never leave off hewing and polishing the living stones, but he, too, is a living stone and is being fitted for his place in the Temple by an even greater builder. The point of view from which he strikes his pedagogical stance is ultimately a limited one and the confidence he may display in his actions is as illusory as the confidence he seeks to undermine. He may succeed in driving his pupils to the discovery of their own insufficiency (ever and always the darkest and deepest point of religion), but he has been driven to the driving and must claim a share of that discovery for himself.

If this is true of Herbert the catechist it is also true of

53. Baynes, *A Commentary*, p. 324. This denial to Peter of the status of "foundation" is a commonplace of Protestant polemics. See Calvin, *Institutes of the Christian Religion*, in *The Library of Christian Classics*, vols. 20 and 21, ed. John T. McNeill, and trans. Ford Lewis Battles (Philadelphia, 1973). Cf. IV: 6. 6.

54. *A Commentary*, p. 325.

Herbert the poet, and the formula devised earlier to account for the presence in his poetry of both order and surprise must now be revised and complicated. That formula was arrived at by transferring the division of labors in Herbert's catechistical theory to the writing and reading of his verse. The poetry is ordered from the perspective of the poet-Questionist who knows from the beginning where he is going (he has the "aim and mark of the whole discourse . . . in his mind"), and it is unpredictable from the perspective of the reader-Answerer who is "driven" by "questions well ordered" to "discover what he is." To the one belongs the stability of an antecedently held and controlling intention, and to the other belongs the realization of that intention, a realization which, because it takes the form of a revelation, will be preceded by uncertainty and restlessness and crowned by surprise. The difficulty with this formula is obvious: while it accommodates the contradictory judgments that have been made of Herbert's poetry, it does so by placing the poet in a position which, in terms of the very lessons he teaches, is reserved solely for God. By granting Herbert the didactic intention that allows him to have both his art and his sincerity, we run the risk of saddling him with a prideful claim. His readers are taught that they must resign the very powers they are exercising, but that obligation extends to the powers he is exercising as well. In short, the order and stability of *The Temple* cannot be attributed to the poet without involving him in the very sin he repeatedly indicts, the sin of playing God.

This does not mean that we must abandon the order/ surprise formula as a way of talking about Herbert's poetry, but that it must be rewritten so as to preserve its usefulness without placing the poet in a false and dangerous position. This can be done by complicating it so that while its terms remain stable in their opposition, the persons attached to those terms shift. Thus from one perspective (to which we are for the most part confined) the reader's uneven career is foreseen and overseen by an omniscient poet-catechist; but from another (of which we get occasional glimpses) the poet himself is the pupil of a higher teacher who overlooks his fumblings with the same benevolent and supervisory intention. In this way the original formula is retained, but in a revised version:

Reader : Herbert   : :   Herbert : God

In short, Herbert stands to God as his readers stand to Herbert. His experience, like ours, is at once contrived (by someone else) and real; that is, it is real for him even if, from a perspective to which he does not have access, its temporal unfolding is an illusion. Herbert himself makes this point in poems whose point is that *he* is not making it. In "The Dedication" he offers the poems as his *"first fruits,"* but then corrects himself: *"Yet not mine neither: for from thee they came"* (line 2). If they are not his, then neither are *their* fruits, the souls they may turn to good: *"Turn their eyes hither, who shall make a gain: | Theirs, who shall hurt themselves or me, refrain"* (lines 5–6). In "The Altar," in "Obedience," in "Jordan II," in "Deniall," in "A True Hymn," in "Praise II," in "The Windows," the exercise of his skill—as poet, preacher, catechist—is inseparable from his resigning of any claim to it and from the realization that the resigning must in turn be resigned. The regress is an infinite one, because whatever position the poet occupies in relation either to his work or to its effects, he finds that position "prepossest." The lesson is read, to us and to himself, many times, but

nowhere so plainly as in "Assurance," a poem whose
title lays claim to the stability that can finally be located
neither in the poet nor in his text:

> Thou art not onely to perform thy part,
> But also mine; as when the league was made
>   Thou didst at once thy self indite,
>   And hold my hand, while I did write.
>   (lines 27–30)

The God who once held his hand (to seal a covenant in
blood) holds it now, writing even those lines that identify
Him as their author. The assurance the speaker finds has
its source neither in his mental nor his verbal structures,
but in an order which they cannot contain even though it
contains, and speaks, them.

We end, then, as we began, with the criticism and its
central question: how is it that a body of poetry can be
characterized as restless and secure at the same time? We
now have two answers to this question, one formal and
intentional, derived directly from Herbert's remarks on
catechizing, and the other an answer that makes the issue
unresolvable in either formal or intentional terms. The
order in the poetry can be explained by attributing to the
poet a conscious aesthetic strategy (to drive the reader to
a deep and dark point of religion), but since the strategy
is one for which he finally cannot claim responsibility, the
explanation dissolves into a mystery (the driving behind
the driving). The dilemma posed by the criticism is removed at one level, but it reappears at another,
reinscribed in a relationship—between the poet and
God—whose dynamics are unavailable to rational
analysis.

It is in fact reinscribed everywhere: having set out to
solve a problem, we have found it to be the content of its

solutions: order and surprise are the constituents of every one of the patterns brought forward to explain their co-presence, and in those patterns the pole that is marked for order is marked, in the context of a wider perspective, for surprise. The temporal experience of Herbert's reader is a function of the poem's spatial (that is, ordered) design, but that design is in turn the working out in time of a design that was made in eternity. The restlessness of individual poems is stabilized in the firm outlines of *The Temple's* structure, but that structure is itself unstable and is left for its true author to finish, in the confidence that he has already finished it. The members of the Church Militant strive to raise themselves into a holy building, but that building already stands in the perfect body of that master-builder who is responsible for their very strivings. The uneven and unpredictable course of self-examination is preliminary to the state of becoming worthy, but that worthiness, rather than being earned is given, and is given by the very host at whose table (always and already set) we come to eat. There are any number of formulas that will allow us to talk about Herbert's poetry, but each of them is a rewriting of the contradiction that exists at its heart, the contradiction between the injunction to do work—to catechize, to raise altars, to edify souls, to rear temples, to write poems— and the realization, everywhere insisted upon, that the work has already been done. It is this contradiction, as it was found in the regular alternations of the criticism, that has impelled this study from the beginning, and here at its conclusion it is with us still. Indeed, one might say that in their failure to resolve it these pages have reproduced it once again.

A Conclusion In Which
It May Appear That
Everything Is Taken Back

MORE THAN once in this book I turn on its argument by pointing out that it has not been demonstrated. The question posed on page 48, "What . . . is my evidence?" marks the first appearance in the book of one of its major strategies, a refusal to rest in the evidence that has been presented so far, and it is a strategy that is pursued at least through the opening sentences of Chapter Three, which begins, "The final piece of evidence is to be found. . . ." On one level, of course, this is a rhetorical ploy, designed to inspire confidence in an author so scrupulous that he repeatedly challenges the force of his own documentation. On another (more important) level, however, it signifies an acceptance on my part of a mode of procedure, along with the assumptions and constraints that are its content. That mode is usually called "literary history" and by every visible sign it is what has been practiced here. The form of my argument, if not its execution, is classic: a problem is identified, in this case the problem of determining what we are to make of the title *The Temple*, and of the sections into which that work is divided; previous efforts to solve the problem are rehearsed and declared to be (at least partial) failures; and hitherto unknown or ignored evidence is brought forward with the claim that in its light all difficulties will fall away and all questions will be answered. In this book that evidence is found in the structures (formal and rhetorical) of the Reformation catechism, and it is to the recovery of those structures (lost, one assumes, because they were so much a part of the landscape as to be the proverbial nose on everyone's face) that I devote most of my expository energies. The unspoken but powerful assumption that gives my performance whatever coherence it has is the assumption of the independence of the evidence from the interpretation it supports. That is, the story which I have been telling has the following plot: an interpretative hunch (that *The Temple* should be regarded as a strategy rather than as an object) is for a time without evidentiary support; an investigation is undertaken in order to see whether support can be found in a body of materials whose form is obviously and indisputably its own (it does not require interpretation); the interpretation and the materials are found to match, and because they match the story ends by certifying itself as a demonstration.

However, it didn't happen that way, and what's more, it never does. What happened was that the shape of both the problem and its solution was a function of the interested perception that I brought to the tasks of scholarship and criticism. The fact that I saw *The Temple* as a strategy was more or less inevitable, given the assumptions (about literature, language, and communication) which constitute the limits of what I can see at all. (One can only read what one has already read.) And it was those same assumptions that led me to give the Reformation catechism the description (a word to be used with the greatest of caution, but, nevertheless, a word that must be used) it has in this book. That description is as much an interpretation as the interpretation it is brought in to support. Indeed, it is the *same* interpretation. Rather than coming upon the conventions of the Reformation catechism and finding them fortuitously available for my interpretive purpose, that purpose was responsible for the shape those conventions already had when they were *first* seen. Indeed they could not have been seen except in the context of some purpose or other; and therefore they were never available in any but an (already) interpreted form. (The past is always a structure seen in the context of the interests of the present and cannot be otherwise seen.) I take this to be a general truth about evidence; it can never confirm an interpretation (if by confirm we mean provide independent support for) because it is always the extension of one. The "facts of the matter" are never simply there waiting to be uncovered by some sufficiently transparent instrument; rather they come into view as a function of categories of understanding which already have a place marked out for them. Since some or other categories of understanding are always operating, there will always be facts, but they will not always be the same ones, and no set of them will have the status that would allow them to be cited as objective and independent proof. This does not mean that a structure of proof cannot be erected, but that its force will be system specific, and that someone who stands outside the system will remain unconvinced because the facts to which the argument refers will not be facts for him. If anyone is persuaded by my reading of *The Temple,* it will not be because he has assented to a disinterested marshaling of facts, but because he has been initiated into a way of seeing as a consequence of which the facts could not be otherwise than I report them. In saying this I might seem to risk undermining the very confidence that I have solicited in the preceding pages. There is no reason, however, why that confidence (if it has been won) should not survive an admission that its basis has been and could only be an act of persuasion rather than an act of demonstration. This is not to oppose persuasion to demonstration, but to assert that the second can occur only if the first has already occurred, and that if the first has in fact occurred the second has occurred already.

Bibliography

PRIMARY SOURCES

The place of publication is London, unless otherwise noted.

A., B. *A treatise of the way to life.* n. d. STC 2.

Abbot, Robert. *Milk for Babes.* 1646. STC 69.

Ainsworth, Henry. *Annotations upon the five books of Moses, the book of the Psalms, and the Song of Songs.* 7 pts. 1627. STC 219.

———. *Certain notes of Mr. Henry Ainsworth, his last sermon. Taken by pen by one of his flock.* 1630. STC 227.

Aldem, Mordecai. *A short catechism.* 1592. STC 287a.

Alleine, Joseph. *A most familiar explanation of the Assemblies shorter catechism. . . . The last edition corrected and much amended.* 1682. Wing A-975.

Alleine, Richard. *A briefe explanation of the common catechisme.* Second ed. 1631. STC 358.

Allen, Robert. *A treasurie of catechisme or christian instruction.* Pt. 1. 1600. STC 366.

Alley, William. *The poore mans librarie.* 1560. STC 375.

Ambrose, Saint. *Theological and Dogmatic Works.* Trans. Roy J. Deferrari. *The Fathers of the Church.* Vol. 44. The Catholic University of America Press, 1963.

———. *Some of the Principal Works.* Trans. H. de Romestin.

Nicene and post-Nicene Fathers of the Christian Church. 2nd ed. Vol. X. New York: The Christian Literature Co., 1896.

Andrewes, Lancelot. *A patterne of catechisticall doctrine.* 1630. STC 603.

———. *A patterne.* 3rd. ed. 1675. Wing A–3148.

———. *XCVI sermons.* Ed. Abp. Laud and Bp. Buckeridge. 1632. STC 606.

The Annotated Book Of Common Prayer. Ed. J. H. Blunt, D. D. New York, 1883.

Apostolical Constitutions. Ante-Nicene Christian Library. Ed. Rev. A. Roberts and J. Donaldson. Vol. XVII. Edinburgh, 1870.

Aquinas, St. Thomas. *The "Summa Theologica" of St. Thomas Aquinas,* literally trans. Fathers of the English Dominican Province. Third number. QQ. LX.-LXXXIII. London: Burns Oates and Washbourne, Ltd., 1913.

Archbold, John. *The beauty of holines. A sermon.* 1621. STC 731.

Augustine, Saint. *De Catechizandis Rudibus.* Ed. G. Kruger. Tübingen, 1934.

———. *De Catechizandis Rudibus.* Trans. and annot. Rev. Joseph P. Christopher. *Ancient Christian Writers.* Vol. II. Westminster, Md.: The Newman Press, 1946.

———. *Easter Sermons.* Ed. Philip Weller. Washington, 1955.

———. *The Teacher.* Trans. and annot. Joseph M. Colleran. *Ancient Christian Writers.* Vol. IX. Westminster, Md.: The Newman Press, 1950.

B., E. *A catechisme with a treatise concerning catechizing.* 1617. STC 1024.

———. *A catechisme or briefe instruction.* 1617.

Babington, Gervase. *Comfortable notes upon the bookes of Numbers and Deuteronomy.* In *The Workes of G. Babington.* 5 pts. 1615. STC 1077.

———. *A profitable exposition of the Lords Prayer.* 1588. STC 1090.

———. *A very fruitfull exposition of the commaundements.* 1583. STC 1095.

———. *A very fruitfull exposition.* Anr. ed. 1596. STC 1098.

Ball, John. *Short questions and answers explaining the catechisme.* 1639. STC 1314.

Basset, William. *A discourse on my lord-archbishop's of Canterbury's . . . letters.* 1684. Wing B–1052.

Bastingius, Jeremias. *A catechisme of christian religion*. 1591. STC 1562.

———. *An exposition or commentarie upon the catechism taught in the Lowe Countryes*. 1589. STC 1564.

———. *An exposition*. Anr. ed. Cambridge. 1595. STC 1566.

Baxter, Richard. *The Catechizing of families, a teacher of housholders how to teach their housholds. Useful also to schoolmasters and tutors of youth. For those that are past the common small catechisms, and would grow to a more rooted faith, and to the fuller understanding of all that is commonly needful to a safe, holy, comfortable and profitable life. Written by Richard Baxter, in hope that family and school-diligence, may do much to keep up true religion*. 1683. Wing B–1205.

———. *The poor man's family book*. 1674. Wing B–1352.

———. *The poor man's family book*. 2nd ed. 1675. Wing B–1353.

———. *The Quakers Catechisme*. 1651. Wing B–1361.

———. *The Quakers Catechisme*. 1656. Wing B–1364.

Baynes, Paul. *A commentarie upon the first chapter of the Epistle to the Ephesians*. 1618. STC 1635.

———. *A commentarie upon the first a. second chapter of S. Paul to the Colossians*. 2 pts. 1634. STC 1636.

———. *A commentary upon the Epistle*. 1642.

———. *An entire commentary upon the whole epistle of the Apostle Paul to the Ephesians*. 1643. Wing B–1549.

Becon, Thomas. *The Catechism of Thomas Becon*. Cambridge, 1844.

———. *The demaundes of holy scripture, with answeres*. 1577. STC 1718.

———. *The governaunce of vertue*. 1549. STC 1725.

———. *The governaunce of vertue*. 1566. STC 1727.

———. *The jewel of joye*. 1553. STC 1733.

Bernard, Richard. *The common catechisme*. 1630. STC 1929.

———. *A double catechisme*. 1607. STC 1936.

———. *Josuahs godly resolution in conference with Caleb*. 1612. STC 1953.

Beze, Theodore de. *A booke of Christian questions and answers*. 1572. STC 2037.

———. *A briefe and pithie summe of the christian faith made in forme of a confession*. 1562–63. STC 2007.

————. *A briefe and pithie summe.* Anr. ed. 1572. STC 2010.

————. *A little catechisme.* 1578. STC 2022.

Biddle, John. *A brief scripture—catechisme for children.* 1654.

————. *Duae Catecheses.* 1664. Wing B–2875.

————. *A twofold catechism.* 1654. Wing B–2882.

The Book of Common Prayer 1559. Ed. J. E. Booty. Charlottesville, 1976.

Boughton, John. *God and man.* 1623. STC 3410.

Bourne, Immanuel. *A light from Christ.* 1645. Wing B–3854.

————. *The true way of a Christian to the new Jerusalem.* 1622. STC 3419.

Boys, John. *An exposition of all the principall scriptures used in our English liturgie.* 1609. STC 3455.

————. *An exposition.* 1610. STC 3456.

Bradshaw, William. *A preparation to receiving the sacrament.* see STC 3511.

————. *Direction for the weaker sort of Christians shewing in what manner they ought to fit themselves to the worthy receiving of the Sacrament. The doctrine of communicating worthily.* 1609. STC 3510.

————. *Directions for the weaker sort.* Anr. ed., pt. 1 rewritten with altered title: *A preparation for receiving the Sacrament. With a profitable treatise.* 5th ed. 1617. STC 3511.

A briefe and necessary catechisme. Very needefull to be knowne of all householders. 1575. STC 4794.

A briefe catechisme. 1576. STC 4798.

A briefe instruction for all families. 1583. STC 21518.

Brinsley, John. *Ludus literarius; or, The grammar schoole.* Ed. E. T. Campagnac. Liverpool and London, 1917.

Browne, Robert. *The Writings of Robert Harrison and Robert Browne.* Ed. Albert Peel and Leland Carlson. London: George Allen and Unwin, 1953.

Browne, Samuel. *The summe of Christian religion.* 1630. STC 3911.

Bucer, Martin. *De Regno Christi.* Ed. W. Pauck. *The Library of Christian Classics.* Vol. 19. Philadelphia, 1969.

Burgesse, Anthony. *The Scripture directory.* 1659. STC 5656.

Burton, Henry. *A briefe catecheticall exposition of christian doctrine.* 1636. STC 4138.

———. *Grounds of Christian religion*. 1631. STC 4143.

———. *Grounds of Christian religion*. 1636. STC 4145.

Butler, Charles. *The English Grammar. Whereunto is annexed an index of words*. 1633. STC 4190.

———. *The English Grammar.* Anr. issue with altered prelimi- nary leaves, including a dedication to Prince Charles. 1634. STC 4191.

Byfield, Nicholas. *A commentary; or sermons upon the second chap- ter of the first epistle of Peter*. 1623. STC 4211.

———. *A commentary upon the three first chapters of the first epistle of Peter*. 3 pts. 1637. STC 4212.

———. *The principall grounds of Christian religion*. 1625. STC 4232.

———. *The rule of faith, or, an exposition of the apostles creed*. 1626. STC 4233.

———. *Sermons upon the first chapter of the first epistle generall of Peter*. 1617. STC 4234.

———. *Sermons upon the ten first verses of the third chapter of the first epistle of Peter*. 1636. STC 4235.

Calvin, Jean. *Catechismus ecclesiae Genevensis*. 1562. STC 4375.

———. *The catechisme or manner to teache children the christian religion*, etc. Geneva. 1556. STC 4380.

———. *The catechisme*. Anr. ed. 1563. STC 4381.

———. *The catechisme*. Anr. ed. 1564. STC 4382.

———. *The catechisme*. 1569. STC 4383.

———. *The catechisme*. 1575. STC 4384.

———. *The catechisme*. 1580. STC 4385.

———. *The catechisme*. 1582. STC 4386.

———. *The catechisme*. 1594. STC 4387.

———. *The catechisme*. 1597. STC 4387a.

———. *The catechisme*. 1602. STC 4388.

———. *The catechisme*. 1611. STC 4389.

———. *The catechisme*. 1628. STC 4390.

———. *Le Catechisme de Geneve*. 1552. STC 4391.

———. *Galatians, Ephesians, Philippians, Colossians. Calvin's New Testament Commentaries*. Trans. T.H. Parker. Eerdmans.

———. *Hebrews and Peter First and Second. Calvin's New Testament Commentaries*. Trans. W.B. Johnson. Eerdmans.

———. *Institutes of the Christian Religion*. Ed. John T. McNeill.

Trans. and indexed Ford Lewis Battles. *The Library of Christian Classics*. Vols. 20 and 21. Philadelphia: The Westminster Press, 6th printing, 1973.

———. *The sermons of John Calvin upon the epistle to the Ephesians*. 1577. STC 4448.

Canisius, Peter. *Ane catechisme or schort instruction of christian religion*. Paris, 1588. STC 4568.

Carter, John. *Winter-evenings communication with young novices*. Cambridge, 1628. STC 4696.

Cartwright, Thomas. *Christian religion substantially treatised*. 1611. STC 5186.

———. *A treatise of Christian religion*. 1616. STC 4313.

———. *Cartwrightiana*. Ed. Albert Peel and Leland Carlson. London: George Allen and Unwin, 1951.

A catechisme in briefe questions and answeres. Oxford, 1629. STC 4800.

A catechisme, or a christian doctrine necessarie for chyldren, etc. Louvain, 1568. STC 4801.

Catechismus ex decreto Conoillii Tridentini ad parochos. Pii. V. et Clementis XIII. Council of Trent, 1545–63.

The Catechism of the Council of Trent. Trans. with notes. 1852.

A Catechism wherein the learner is at once taught to rehearse, and prove all the main points of Christian religion, by answering to every question in the very words of Holy Scripture. Together with a . . . discourse . . . of the being of a God and the truth of Scripture. 1674.

Cawdrey, Robert. *A short and fruitfull treatise of the profite of catechising*. 1580. STC 4882.

———. *A treasurie or store-house of similes*. 1600. STC 4887.

Certayne short questions and answers . . . in the principles of the christian faith. 1580. STC 20558.

Charcke, William. *Of the use of catechising*. 1580. See Cawdrey, 1580.

Chrysostom, St. John. *An exposition upon the epistle to the Ephesians*. 1581. STC 14632.

———. *Baptismal Instructions*. Trans. Paul W. Harkins. *Ancient Christian Writers*. Vol. XXXI. Westminster, Md.: The Newman Press, 1963.

———. *Homilies*. Ed. John Henry Parker. Oxford, 1845.

Chub, William. *The true travaile of all faithfull Christians.* 1585. STC 5211.

———. *Two fruitefull and godly sermons.* 1585. STC 5212.

Clapham, Henoch. *A briefe of the Bible drawne into English poesy.* 1596. STC 5332.

Clement of Alexandria. *Christ the Educator.* Trans. Simon P. Wood. *The Fathers of the Church.* Vol. 23, New York: Fathers of the Church, Inc., 1954.

———. *Le Pédagogue.* Livre I. Intro. et notes Henri-Irénée Marrow. Traduction de Marguerite Harl. *Sources Chrétiennes.* No. 70. Paris: Les éditions du Cerf, 1960.

———. *Le Pédagogue.* Livre II. Traduction de Claude Mondésert. Notes de Henri-Irénée Marrow. *Sources Chrétiennes.* No. 108. Paris: Les éditions du Cerf, 1965.

———. *Le Pédagogue.* Livre III. Traduction de Claude Mondésert et Chantal Matray. Notes de Henri-Irénée Marrow. *Sources Chrétiennes.* No. 158. Paris: Les éditions du Cerf, 1970.

The Clementine Homilies. Ante-Nicene Christian Library. Vol. XVII. Edinburgh, 1870.

Cobhead, Thomas. *A briefe instruction for the exercise of youth.* 1579. STC 5455.

Coles, William. *The art of simpling.* 1656. Wing C–5089.

Comber, Thomas. *A companion to the temple: or, A helpe to devotion, in the daily use of the common-prayer.* In two parts, The third edition with additions. 1679. Wing C–5454.

Compton, Henry. *The Bishop of London, his letter to the clergy.* 1679. Wing C–5669.

Cooper, C. *The English Teacher.* 1687. Wing C–6051.

Coote, Edmund. *The Englishe scholemaister.* 1596. STC 5711.

———. *The Englishe scholemaister.* Anr. ed. 1614. STC 5712.

Craig, John. *A short summe of the whole catechisme.* 1581. STC 5962.

Cranmer, Thomas. *Catechismus. That is to say; a shorte instruction into Christian religion.* 1548. STC 5993.

———. *Catechismus. That is to say; a shorte instruction into Christian religion.* Anr. ed. 1548. STC 5994.

Crashaw, Richard. *Crashaw's Poetical Works.* Ed. L. C. Martin.

Oxford, 1927.

Crashaw, William. *Milke for babes, or a north-countrie catechisme.* 2nd ed. 1618. STC 6020.

———. *Milke for babes.* Anr. ed. 1622. STC 6021.

Crewe, Thomas. *The nosegay of morall philosophie.* 1580. STC 6039.

Crompton, William. *An explication of those principles of Christian religion exprest in the booke of Common Prayer.* 1633. STC 6057.

Crooke, Samuel. *The guide unto true blessednesse. A brief direction to true happiness.* 2 pts. 1613. STC 6066.

———. *The guide unto true blessednesse.* 6th ed. 1640. STC 6068.

Cyprian. *Letters* 1-81. Trans. Sister Rose Bernard Donna, C.S.J. *The Fathers of the Church.* Vol. 51. The Catholic University of America Press, 1964.

Cyril of Jerusalem. *Catacheses Illuminatorum Hierosolymis XVIII et quinque mystagogicae . . . nunc primum Latinate donatae in lucem prodeunt.* Ioanne Gredecio. Coloniae: Apud Maternum Cholinum, 1564.

Cyrille de Jérusalem. *Catecheses Mystagogiques.* Introd., texte critique et notes de Auguste Piédagnel. Traduction de Pierre Paris, P.S.S. Paris: Les éditions du Cerf, 1966.

Cyril of Jerusalem. *Works.* 2 vols. Trans. Leo P. McCauley and Anthony A. Stephenson. *The Fathers of the Church.* Vols. 61, 64. The Catholic University Press of America, 1970.

Daines, Simon. *Orthoepeia Anglicana: or the first part of the English Grammar,* etc. 1640. STC 6190.

Day, John. *Day's dyall or, his twelve howres, that is twelve lectures by way of catechisme.* 1614. STC 6425.

Démonstration de le Prédication Apostolique. Ed. and trans. L. M. Froidevaux. Paris, 1959.

Denison, Stephen. *A compendious catechisme.* The third impression. 1621. STC 6599.

Dent, Arthur. *A pastime for parents contayning the grounds of christian religion.* 1606. STC 6622.

———. *A plain exposition of the articles of our faith, by short questions and answeres, for the understanding of the simple.* 1594. STC 6625a.

———. *The plaine mans path-way to Heaven.* 1601. STC 6626.

————. *The plaine mans path-way to Heaven*. Anr. ed. 1603.

Dering, Edward. *A brief & necessary instruction, verye needeful to bee knowen of all housholders*. 1572. STC 6679.

————. *A brief and necessary instruction*. Anr. ed. *A briefe and necessarie catechisme*. 1597. STC 6681.

————. *A short catechisme for householders. With prayers to the same adjoyning*. 1582. STC 6711.

————. *Maister Derings Workes*. 1590. STC 6676.

Dickenson, William. *Milke for babes. The Eng. Catechisme explaned*. (Init. W. D.) 1628. STC 6822.

The Didache. Trans. and annot. James A. Kleist, S.J. *Ancient Christian Writers*. Vol. VI. Westminster, Md.: The Newman Press, 1948.

Didascalia Apostolorum. The Syrian version translated and accompanied by the Verona Latin fragments, with introd. and notes R. Hugh Connolly. Oxford: Clarendon Press, 1969.

Dod, John. *A plain and familiar exposition of the ten commandments*. 19th ed. 1662. Wing D–1786 B.

Donne, John. *Sermons*. Ed. George R. Potter and Evelyn M. Simpson. Berkeley and Los Angeles: University of California Press, 1953–62.

Duncan, Andrew. *Rudimenta pietatis*. 1595. STC 7352.

E., G. *The Christian schoole-maister*. 1613. STC 7433.

Edgeworth, Roger. *Sermons very fruitfull, godly, and learned*. 1557. STC 7482.

Egerton, Stephen. *A briefe methode of catechizing: the sixteenth edition*. 1610. STC 7528.

Elton, Edward. *A forme of catechizing*. 1616. STC 7615.

————. *A forme of catechizing*. 9th ed. 1629. STC 7617.

Etheria. *Peregrinatio Etheriae*. (see Duchesne, L., secondary sources.)

Facsimile of The Black-letter Prayer-book of 1636. Southampton, 1870.

Featley, Daniel. *The summe of saving knowledge*. 1626. STC 10739.

Fenton, Edward. *So short a catechism, that whosoever wil not learne are not to be admitted to the Lord's Supper*. 1626. STC 10788.

————. *So short a catechisme*. 1641. Wing F–718.

The Ferrar Papers. Ed. B. Blackstone. Cambridge, 1938.

Nicholas Ferrar: Two Lives by his Brother John and by Doctor Jebb. Ed. J. E. B. Mayor, being part 1 of *Cambridge in the Seventeenth Century.* Cambridge, 1855.

Field, Theophilus. *A Christians preparation to the worthy receiving of the Lords supper.* 1622. STC 10860.

———. *A Christians preparation.* Anr. ed. *Parasceve Paschae: or a christians preparation to receiving of the Lords supper.* 1624. STC 10861.

Ford, Simon. *A short catechism declaring the practical use of the covenant interest, and baptism of the infant seed of believers. Being extracted out of two dialogues concerning that subject.* With an epistle annexed by the Rev. Dr. [Edward] Reynolds. 1657. Wing F-502.

F., I. or J. (Fotherby, I. or J.) *The covenant betweene God and Man.* 1616. STC 10639.

Foxe, John. *A most breefe manner of instruction to the principles of christian religion.* 1550. STC 11238.

Frewen, John. *Certaine choise grounds, and principles of our Christian religion,* etc. 1621. STC 11379.

G., I. or J. *The Christians profession, or a treatise of the grounds of divinity,* etc. 1630. STC 11498.

Gibson, John. *An easie entrance into the principall points of christian religion.* 1579. STC 11832.

———. *An easie entrance.* 1581. STC 11833.

Gomersall, Robert. *Sermons on St. Peter.* 1634. STC 11994.

Gouge, William. *A short catechisme.* 1615. STC 12126.

Graie, H. *A short and easie introduction to christian faith.* 1588. STC 12170.

Gregory, Bishop of Nyssa. Ascetical Works. Trans. Virginia Woods Callahan. *The Fathers of the Church.* Vol. 58. The Catholic University of America Press, 1967.

———. *Select Writings and Letters.* Trans. with prolegomena, notes, and indices by William Moore and Henry Austin Wilson. *Nicene and Post-Nicene Fathers.* Vol. V. New York: The Christian Literature Co., 1893.

Grotius, Hugo. *De veritate religionis christianae.* Editio quinta, auctior. 1639. STC 12399.

———. *The English version of Hugo Grotius his catechisme.* 1668. Wing G–2110.

————. *Hugo Grotius de veritate religionis Christianae.* 1650. Wing G–2100.

H., R. *Three formes of catechismes.* 1583. STC 12575.

Hall, Joseph. *The Works of Joseph Hall . . . with a table newly added to the whole worke.* 1628. STC 12637c.

————. *The Works. . . .* Arranged and rev. Joseph Pratt. London, 1808.

Harris, Edmond. *A sermon preached at Hitchin.* 1590. STC 12804.

Harrison, Robert. *The Writings of Robert Harrison and Robert Browne.* Ed. Albert Peel and Leland H. Carlson. London: George Allen and Unwin, 1953.

Heidelberg Catechism. The catechisme, or maner to teach children. 1572. STC 13028.

Heidelberg Catechism. A catechisme or short kind of instruction. Oxford. 1588. STC 13030.

Hemmingsen, Niels. *The Epistle of the Blessed Apostle.* 1580.

————. *The epistle to the Ephesians expounded.* 1580. STC 13058.

Herbert, George. *The Poems of George Herbert.* Introd. Helen Gardner. London: Oxford University Press, 1961.

————. *The Works of George Herbert.* Ed. with a commentary F. E. Hutchinson. 1941; rpt. Oxford: Clarendon Press, 1959.

————. *The English Works of George Herbert.* Ed. G.H. Palmer. 3 vols. Cambridge, Mass., 1905.

————. *The English Poems of George Herbert.* Ed. C. A. Patrides. London: Dent, 1974.

————. *The Selected Poetry of George Herbert.* Ed. Joseph H. Summers. New York: New American Library, 1967.

Hieron, Samuel. *The doctrine of the beginning of Christ.* 6th ed. 1613. STC 13400.

————. *The doctrine of the beginning of Christ.* 13th ed. 1626. STC 13403.

Hill, William. *The first principles of a Christian.* 1616. STC 13503.

Hinde, William. *A path to pietie.* 1613. STC 13515.

Hodges, Richard. *The English Primrose.* 1664. Wing H–2311.

Holland, Henry. *The historie of Adam.* 1606. STC 13587.

Hooker, Richard. *Of the Lawes of Ecclesiasticall Politie.* facsim. London, 1594. Da Capo Press, 1971.

Hopkinson, William. *A preparation into the waye of lyfe.* 1581. STC 13774.

Horne, William. *A Christian exercise, containing an easie entrance into the principles of religion.* 1580 (?). STC 13826.

Horton Thomas. *Wisdome's judgment of folly.* 1653. Wing H–2884.

Irénée de Lyon. *Démonstration de la Predication Apostolique.* Traduction de l'Arménien avec introd. et notes par L. M. Froidevaux. *Sources Chrétiennes.* No. 62. Paris: Les éditions du Cerf, 1959.

Jewel, John. *Works.* Ed. Richard William Jelf. 8 vols. Oxford University, 1848.

Jones, Richard. *A briefe a. necessarie catechisme.* 1583. STC 14729.

Justin Martyr. *Writings.* Trans. Thomas B. Falls. *The Fathers of the Church.* Vol. I. New York: Christian Heritage, Inc., 1948.

Ken, Thomas. *An exposition on the church-catechism, or the practice of divine love, revised.* Composed for the diocese of Bath and Wells. 1686. Wing K–261.

L., W. *Helpe for young people.* 1649. Wing L–87.

Laud, William. *The Works of the Most Reverend Father in God: William Laud, sometimes Lord Archbishop of Canterbury.* 7 vols., 1860. AMS Press.

Lee, Samuel. *Orbis miraculum, or the Temple of Solomon.* 1659. Wing L–900.

Leech, James. *A plaine and profitable catechisme,* etc. 1605. STC 15365.

LeMacon, Robert. *Catechisme et instruction familiere pour les enfans, qui se preparent à commiquer à la sainte Cene,* 1602. STC 15449.

———. *A catechisme and playne instruction for children, which prepare theseselves to communicate. According to the order of the Frenche church at London.* 1580. STC 15450.

Leo I, Pope. *Letters.* Trans. Edmund Hunt. *The Fathers of the Church.* Vol. 34. New York: Fathers of the Church, Inc., 1957.

Littleton, Edmund. *A briefe catechisme, containing the summe of the gospels.* 1631. STC 15718.

Luther, Martin. *Catecheses D. Martini Lutheri minor Germanice, Latine, Graece, et Ebraice.* Edita studio et opera M. Johannis Claii Hertzberg. Iterum recognita et emendata. Witebergae, 1578.

——. *The small catechism*. Literally trans. Trans. rev. and corr. Rev. H. Wetzel, 1872. In *Ecclesiastical Various*. Vol. 39. The Library of the Johns Hopkins University.

——. *Works*. Vol. II. Philadelphia: Muhlenberg Press, 1943.

Lye, Thomas. *The Assemblies shorter catechism*. 1674. Wing L–3528.

——. *The Childs Delight*. 1675. Wing L–3530.

——. *An explanation of the shorter catechism*. 1675 Wing L–3532.

Lyster, John. *A rule how to bring up children*. 1558. STC 17122.

Masterson, George. *The Spiritual House*. 1661. Wing M–1073.

Mayer, John. *The English catechisme; or a commentarie*, etc. 1621. STC 17732.

——. *The English catechisme*. 2nd ed. 1622. STC 17733.

——. *Mayers catechisme abridged*. 2nd ed. 1623. STC 17739.

Micron, Marten. *A short and faythful instruction for symple christianes whych intende worthely to receyve the holy Supper*. 1560. STC 17864.

Mulcaster, Richard. *Catechismus Paulinus*. 1601. STC 18249.

Niceta of Remesiana. *Writings*. Trans. Gerald G. Walsh, S.J. *The Fathers of the Church*. Vol. 7. New York: Fathers of the Church, Inc., 1949.

Nicholes, M. *A catechisme*. 1631. STC 18531.

Nixon, Anthony. *The dignitie of man*. 1612. STC 18584.

Nowell, Alexander. *A catechisme, or institution of christian religion, to bee learned of all youth next after the little catechisme, appointed in the Booke of Common Prayer*. 1572. STC 18730.

——. *A catechisme*. 1593. STC 18733.5.

——. *A catechisme*. 1614. STC 18735.

——. *A Catechism Written in Latin by Alexander Nowell, Dean of St. Paul's Together with the Same Catechism Translated into English by Thomas Norton*. Ed. G. E. Corrie. Cambridge, 1853.

Oley, Barnabas. *Herbert's Remains, or, Sundry pieces of that sweet singer of the Temple, Mr. George Herbert, sometime orator of the University of Cambridge. Now exposed to publick light*. 1652.

Openshaw, Robert. *Short questions and answears conteyning the summe of christian religion*. 1579. STC 18816.

——. *Short questions*. 1617. STC 18824.

Origen. *Contra Celsum.* Translated, with an introduction and notes by Henry Chadwick. Cambridge University Press, 1953.

———. *Contra Celse.* Tome I. Introd., texte critique, traduction et notes Marcel Borret, S.J. *Sources Chrétiennes.* No. 132.

———. *Contra Celse.* Tome II. Introd., texte critique, traduction et notes Marcel Borret, S.J. *Sources Chrétiennes.* No. 136. Paris: Les éditions du Cerf, 1968.

Owen, John. *Vindiciae evangelicae or the mystery.* 1655. Wing O–823.

P., O. *Vocal Organ.* Oxford, 1665. Wing P–3396.

Paget, John. *A primer of christian religion.* 1601. STC 19100.

Palmer, Herbert. *An endeavor of making.* 3rd ed. 1644. Wing P–230a.

Pasquier, Etienne. *The Jesuites catechisme.* 1602. STC 19449.

Perkins, William. *The foundation of Christian religion.* 1590. STC 19709.

———. *The foundation of Christian religion.* Anr. ed. 1615. STC 19715a.

Pinner, Charles. *Two sermons at Marleburgh.* (On Peter ii. 17.) 1597. STC 19946.

Plato. *The Collected Dialogues.* Ed. Edith Hamilton and H. Cairns. Princeton, 1963.

Poole, Matthew. *Annotations Upon the Holy Bible.* 1683. Wing P–2820.

———. *Annotations Upon the Holy Bible.* 3rd. ed. 2 vols. 1696. Wing P–2824.

Poynet, John. *Catechismus brevis, christianae discipline summam continens, omnibus ludi magistris authoritate regia commendatus. Huic catechismo adiuncti sunt Articuli,* etc. Compiled, probably by John Poynet, and set forth by royal authority. 1553. STC 4807.

The Presbyterian Movement in the Reign of Queen Elizabeth, as Illustrated by the Minute Book of the Dedham Classics 1582-1589. Ed. Roland G. Usher. London: Offices of the Royal Historical Society, 1905.

Presse, Simon. *A sermon preached at Egginton.* 1597. STC 20207.

Preston, Richard. *The doctrine of the lords supper.* 1621. STC 20283.

————. *Short questions and answers explaining the use of the Sacraments,* etc. 1621. STC 20286.

Randall, John. *Three and twentie sermons, or catechisticall lectures upon the Sacrament of the Lords Supper.* 1630. STC 20682.

Ratcliffe, Thomas. *A short summe of the whole catechisme for the greater ease of the common people of Saint Saveries in Southwarke.* 1619. STC 20746.

Rogers, Daniel. *A practicall catechisme.* 1632. STC 21166.

Rogers, John. *The summe of Christianitie.* 1560. STC 21183.

Rouspeau, Yves. *A treatise of the preparation to the holy supper.* 1578. STC 21352.

————. *A treatise.* Anr. ed. 1579. STC 21353.

Ryley, George. (see Heissler, J.M., secondary sources)

Sanderson, Robert. *Two sermons.* (On I Peter ii. 16 and Rom. xiv. 23). 1635. STC 21710.

————. *XXXVI Sermons.* 8th ed. 1689. STC 639.

Sclater, William, the elder. *An exposition with notes upon the first epistle to the Thessalonians.* 2 vols. 1627. STC 21835.

————. *A key to the key of Scripture: or an exposition with notes on the three first chapters of the Epistle to the Romans.* 1611. STC 21838.

————. *A key to the key. . . .* 2nd. ed. 1629. STC 21840.

A short catechisme, or playne instruction, conteyning the sume of christian learninge, sett fourth for all scholemaisters to teache. To thys catechisme are adjoyned the Articles. 1553. STC 4812.

Shutte, Christopher. *The testimonie of a true fayth.* 1577. STC 22467.

Smith, John. *Essex dove presenting the world with a few of her olive branches.* 1629. STC 22798.

Sparke, Thomas. *A catechism or short kind of instruction,* etc. 1588. STC—see listings under Heidelberg catechism.

————. *A short treatise, very comfortable,* etc. *(A brief and short catechisme).* 2 pts. 1580. STC 23025.

————. *A treatise to prove that Ministers are bound to catechise.* 1588.

Sprint, John. *The summe of the christian religion.* 1613. STC 23111.

Stephens, Edward. *The liturgy of the ancients.* 1696. Wing S–5429.

————. *The apology of Socrates Christianus.* 1700. Wing S–5418a.

Stockwood, John. *A short catechisme for householders; gathered by J. Stockwood.* 1582. See Cawdrey, 1580.

Syme, John. *The sweet milke of christian doctrine.* 1617. STC 23585.

Taverner, Richard. *A catechisme or institution of the Christian religion.* 1539. STC 23709.

Taylor, Jeremy. *The Whole Works, . . . with an essay, biographical and critical.* London, 1835.

Tertullian. *Disciplinary, Moral, and Ascetical Works.* Trans. Rudolph Arbesmann, O.S.A., Sister Emily Joseph Daly, C.S.J., Edwin A. Quain, S.J. *The Fathers of the Church.* Vol. 40. New York: Fathers of the Church, Inc., 1959.

———. *Treatises on Penance; on Penitence and Purity.* Trans. and annot. William P. Le Saint, S.J. *Ancient Christian Writers.* Vol. XXVIII. Westminster, Md.: The Newman Press, 1959.

Théodore de Mopsueste. *Les Homélies Catéchétiques.* Traduction, introduction, index Raymond Tonneau et Robert Devreesse. Biblioteca Apostolica Vaticana, MDCCCCXLIX.

———. "Synopsis of Christian Doctrine in the Fourth Century According to Theodore of Mopsuestia," ed. Alphonse Mingana. *Bulletin of the John Rylands Library* 5 (Aug. 1918–July 1920), 296–316.

Tombes, John. *Anthropolatria; or, the sinne.* 1645. Wing S–1796.

The Treatise on the Apostolic Tradition of St. Hippolytus of Rome. Ed. Gregory Dix. London, 1968.

Twisse, William. *A briefe catecheticall exposition of christian doctrine.* 1632. STC 24400.

Tymme, Thomas. *A commentarie upon S. Paules epistles to the Corinthians . . . translated . . . into Englishe, by Thomas Tymme.* 1577.

Vaughan, Henry. *The Works of Henry Vaughan.* Ed. L. C. Martin. Oxford, 1957.

Vesey, Henry. *The scope of the scripture.* 1621. STC 24694.

Vicars, Thomas. *The grounds of that doctrine which is according to godlinesse,* etc. 1630. STC 24700.

———. *The grounds.* 3rd ed. 1631. STC 24701.

Walkington, Thomas. *An exposition of the two first verses of the sixt chapter to the Hebrewes (Two sermons, etc.).* 1609. STC 24966. 24966.

Walton, Izaak. *The lives of.* 4th ed. 1675. Wing W–672.

————. *The Life of Mr. George Herbert.* 1670. In *World's Classics* ed. 1927; rpt. London, 1970, 1973.

————. *The Lives of Dr. John Donne, Sir Henry Wotton, Mr. Richard Hooker, Mr. George Herbert.* 1670.

Warford, William. *A briefe instruction by way of dialogue concerninge the principall poyntes of christian religion.* 1604. STC 25068.

————. *A briefe instruction. . . .* Anr. ed. 1616. STC 25069.

Watson, Christopher. *Briefe principles of religion, for the exercise of youth.* 1581. STC 25110.

Westfaling, Herbert. *A treatise of reformation in religion.* 1582. STC 25285.

Westminster Assembly of Divines. *The humble advice of the Assembly of Divines, sitting at Westminster, concerning a larger and a shorter catechisme.* 1648. Wing W–1438.

Whitaker, William. *A short summe of christianity.* 1630. STC 25369.

White, Josias. *A plaine and familiar exposition upon the creed.* 1637. STC 25400.

Whiting, Giles. *Short questions and answeres to be learned of such as be ignorant.* 1613. STC 25434.

Wilkinson, Henry. *A catechisme for the use of the congregation of Wadston.* 2nd. ed. 1624. STC 25644.

Williams, John. *A catechism truly representing the doctrines and practices of the Church of Rome, with an answer thereunto. By a Protestant of the Church of England.* 1686. Wing W-2693.

SECONDARY SOURCES

Addleshaw, G. *The Architectural Setting of Anglican Worship.* London: Faber and Faber, 1950.

Asals, Heather. "The Voice of George Herbert's 'The Church.'" *ELH* 36 (1969), 511–528.

Blau, S. D. *Texts and Contexts: Studies Toward a Reading of George Herbert.* Diss. Brandeis, 1967.

Bouyer, Louis. *Liturgy and Architecture.* Notre Dame, Ind.: University of Notre Dame Press, 1967.

Bromiley, G.W. *Baptism and the Anglican Reformers.* London: Lutterworth Press, 1953.

Bush, Douglas. *English Literature in the Earlier Seventeenth Century.* Oxford University Press, 1945.

Carnes, Valerie. "The Unity of George Herbert's *The Temple:* A Reconsideration." *ELH* 35 (1968), 505–526.

The Catholic Encyclopedia. 15 vols. and index. New York: The Encyclopedia Press, 1913.

Clark, Ira. " 'Lord, in thee the Beauty Lies in the Discovery': 'Love Unknown' and Reading Herbert," *ELH* 39 (1972), 560–584.

Clements, A. L. "Theme, Tone, and Tradition in George Herbert's Poetry." *ELR* 3 (1973), 264–283.

Colie, Rosalie. *Paradoxica Epidemica: The Renaissance Tradition of Paradox.* Princeton: Princeton University Press, 1966.

Coolidge, John S. *The Pauline Renaissance in England: Puritanism and the Bible.* Oxford: Clarendon Press, 1970.

Curtis, S.J. *History of Education in Great Britain.* London, 1965.

Cyclopedia of Biblical, Theological, and Ecclesiastical Literature. New York, 1868.

Daniélou, Jean. *The Bible and the Liturgy.* Notre Dame, Ind.: University of Notre Dame Press, 1956.

—— and Régine du Charlat. *La Catéchèse aux Premiers Siècles.* Paris: Fayard-Mame, 1968.

Davies, Horton. *Worship and Theology in England: From Cranmer to Hooker.* Princeton, 1970.

——. *Worship and Theology in England: From Andrewes to Baxter and Fox.* Princeton, 1975.

Devreesse, Robert. *Essai sur Théodore de Mopsueste.* Biblioteca Apostolica Vaticana, MDCCCCXXXXVIII.

Dix, Gregory. *The Shape of the Liturgy.* 2nd ed. Allenson, 1945.

Doerkson, D. W. *Conflict and Resolution in George Herbert's The Temple.* Diss. Univ. of Wisconsin, 1973.

Drake, B. *The Patterning of George Herbert's The Temple (1633): Critics and Manuscripts.* Diss. University of Illinois, 1966.

Duchesne, L. *Christian Worship: Its Origin and Evolution.* London, 1904.

Eames, Wilberforce. *Early New England Catechisms.* In *American Antiquarian Society Proceedings,* Worcester, Massachusetts. 1899. Reissued Detroit: Singing Tree Press, 1969.

Endicott, Annabel M. "The Structure of George Herbert's *Temple:* A Reconsideration." *UTQ* 34 (1965), 226–237.

Fish, Stanley E. "Catechizing the Reader: Herbert's Socratean Rhetoric." In *The Rhetoric of Renaissance Poetry from Wyatt to Milton.* Ed. Thomas O. Sloan and Raymond B. Waddington. Berkeley and Los Angeles: University of California Press, 1974, pp. 174–188.

———. "Letting Go: The Reader in Herbert's Poetry." *ELH* 37 (1970), 475–494.

———. *Self-Consuming Artifacts: The Experience of Seventeenth-Century Literature.* Berkeley and Los Angeles: University of California Press, 1972.

Ford, B. *The Influence of the Prayer Book Calendar on the Shape of George Herbert's The Temple.* Diss. Virginia, 1964.

Freeman, Rosemary. *English Emblem Books.* 1948. Rpt. New York: Octagon Books, 1966.

Freer, Coburn. *Music for a King: George Herbert's Style and the Metrical Psalms.* Baltimore: The Johns Hopkins University Press, 1972.

Grierson, H. J. C., ed. *Metaphysical Lyrics & Poems of the Seventeenth Century.* Oxford, 1921.

Halewood, William H. *The Poetry of Grace: Reformation Themes and Structures in English Seventeenth-Century Poetry.* New Haven and London: Yale University Press, 1970.

Hanley, Sister S. W. *The Unity of George Herbert's The Temple.* Diss. Notre Dame, 1966.

Hardison, Jr., O. B. *Christian Rite and Christian Drama in the Middle Ages: Essays in the Origin and Early History of Modern Drama.* Baltimore: The Johns Hopkins University Press, 1965.

Harman, Barbara Leah. "George Herbert's 'Affliction (I)': Autobiography and Devotion." *ELH* 1977 (forthcoming).

Heissler, John Martin. *Mr. Herbert's Temple and Church Militant Explained and Improved by a Discourse Upon Each Poem Critical and Practical by George Ryley: A Critical Edition.* 2 pts. Diss. University of Illinois, 1960.

Johnson, Lee Ann. "The Relationship of 'The Church Militant' to *The Temple.*" *SP* 67 (1971), 200–206.

Jungmann, Josef A. *The Early Liturgy.* Trans. Francis A. Brunner. Notre Dame, Ind.: University of Notre Dame Press, 1959.

———. *Missarum sollemnia eine genetische Erklarung der romischen messe.* Wien, Herder, 1949.

Leclercq, H. *Dictionnaire D'Archéologie Chretienne et De Liturgie.* Ed. R. P. Chabrol et al. Paris, 1910.

Lewalski, Barbara K. "Typology and Poetry: A Consideration of Herbert, Vaughn, and Marvell." In *Illustrious Evidence: Approaches to English Literature of the Early Seventeenth-Century.* Ed., with introd., Earl Miner. Berkeley and Los Angeles: University of California Press, 1975, pp. 41–69.

McCanles, Michael. *Dialectical Criticism and Renaissance Literature.* Berkeley and Los Angeles: University of California Press, 1975.

McLaughlin, Elizabeth and Gail Thomas. "Communion in *The Temple.*" *SEL* XV (1975), 110–124.

Markus, R.A., ed. *Augustine: A Collection of Critical Essays.* Garden City, New York: Anchor Books, 1972.

Martz, Louis. "The Action of the Self: Devotional Poetry in the Seventeenth Century." In *Metaphysical Poetry, Stratford-Upon-Avon Studies* 11. Ed. Malcolm Bradbury and David Palmer. New York, 1970, pp. 101–121.

———, ed. *The Meditative Poem: An Anthology of Seventeenth-Century Verse.* Garden City, New York: Anchor Books, 1963.

———. *The Poetry of Meditation: A Study in English Religious Literature of the Seventeenth Century.* New Haven: Yale University Press, 1954.

Maycock, A.L. *Nicholas Ferrar of Little Gidding.* London, 1938.

Mills, Jerry Leach. "Recent Studies in Herbert." *ELR* 6 (1976), 105–118.

Miner, Earl. *The Metaphysical Mode from Donne to Cowley.* Princeton: Princeton University Press, 1969.

Montgomery, Robert. "The Province of Allegory in George Herbert's Verse." *TSLL* 1 (1960), 457–72.

Mulder, John R. *The Temple of the Mind: Education and Literary Taste in Seventeenth-Century England.* New York: Western Publishing, Inc., 1969.

Patrick, J. Max. "Critical Problems in Editing George Herbert's

The Temple." In *The Editor as Critic and the Critic as Editor.* Ed. Murray Krieger. William Andrews Clark Memorial Library, 1973, pp. 3–40.

Paynter, Sister Maria de Ricci. *The Churches Banquet: A Study of George Herbert's The Temple.* Diss. Wisconsin, 1965.

Pettit, Norman. *The Heart Prepared: Grace and Conversion in Puritan Spiritual Life.* New Haven and London: Yale University Press, 1966.

Poggi, Valentina. *George Herbert.* Bologna, 1967.

Ray, R.H. *George Herbert in the Seventeenth Century: Allusions to Him, Collected and Annotated.* Diss. Texas, 1967.

Rickey, Mary Ellen. *Utmost Art: Complexity in the Verse of George Herbert.* Lexington: University of Kentucky Press, 1966.

Rieu, M. *Catechetics* (Chicago, 1927).

Simon, Joan. *Education And Society In Tudor England.* Cambridge, 1966.

Smithson, Bill. "Herbert's 'Affliction' Poems." *SEL* 15 (1975), 125–140.

Stambler, Elizabeth. "The Unity of Herbert's *Temple.*" *Cross-Currents* 13 (1960), 251–266.

Stein, Arnold. *George Herbert's Lyrics.* Baltimore: The Johns Hopkins University Press, 1968.

Stewart, Stanley. "Time and *The Temple.*" *SEL* 6 (1966), 97–110.

Summers, Joseph H. *George Herbert: His Religion and Art.* 1954. Rpt. Cambridge, Mass.: Harvard University Press, 1968.

Swardson, H. R. *Poetry and the Fountain of Light: Observations on the Conflict between Christian and Classical Traditions in Seventeenth-Century Poetry.* Columbia: University of Missouri Press, 1962.

Thorpe, James. "Reflections and Self-Reflections: Outlandish Proverbs as a Context for George Herbert's Other Writings." In *Illustrious Evidence: Approaches to English Literature of the Early Seventeenth Century.* Ed., with an introd., Earl Miner. Berkeley and Los Angeles: University of California Press, 1975, pp. 23–37.

Turck, André. *Évangélisation et Catéchèse aux deux premiers siècles.* Paris: Les éditions du Cerf, 1962.

Tuve, Rosemond. "George Herbert and *Caritas.*" 1959. In *Essays by Rosemond Tuve: Spenser, Herbert, Milton.* Ed. Thomas P. Roche, Jr. Princeton: Princeton University Press, 1970, pp. 167–206.

————. *A Reading of George Herbert.* Chicago: University of Chicago Press, 1952.

————. "Sacred 'parody' of Love Poetry, and Herbert." In *Essays.* Ed. Roche. Pp. 207–249.

Vendler, Helen. *The Poetry of George Herbert.* Cambridge and London: Harvard University Press, 1975.

————. "The Re-invented Poem: George Herbert's Alternatives." In *Forms of Lyric.* Ed., with foreword, Reuben Brower. New York and London: Columbia University Press, 1970, pp. 19–45.

Wainwright, Geoffrey. *Christian Initiation. Ecumenical Studies.* No. 10.

Walker, John. "The Architectonics of George Herbert's *The Temple.*" *ELH* 29 (1962), 289–305.

Wedgwood, C. V. *Seventeenth-Century English Literature.* Oxford, 1950.

Westfall, Richard S. *Science and Religion in Seventeenth-Century England.* New Haven: Yale University Press, 1958.

Westgate, S.S. *Delight into Sacrifice: Instructional Modes in George Herbert's Temple.* Diss. University of California, Berkeley, 1972.

Whitaker, Edward. *Documents of the Baptismal Liturgy.* London, 1960.

White, Helen C. *The Metaphysical Poets: A Study in Religious Experience.* 1936. Rpt. New York: Collier Books, 1962.

White, R. E. O. *The Biblical Doctrine of Initiation.* London, 1960.

Williamson, George. *The Donne Tradition.* Noonday Press edition, New York, 1958.

INDEX OF AUTHORS